Marriage:
SINK OR SWIM

Marriage:
SINK OR SWIM

Chapters from Cheryl Petersen's, *"21st Century Science and Health with Key to the Scriptures"* (4th edition), a revision of Mary Baker Eddy's "*Science and Health*."

Healing Science Today

Unless otherwise footnoted, Scripture taken from the HOLY BIBLE, NEW INTERNATIONAL
VERSION ®. Copyright © 1973, 1978, 1984 by International Bible Society. Used by permission of
Zondervan. All rights reserved. (www.Zondervan.com)Verses marked "NASB" are taken from the
NEW AMERICAN STANDARD BIBLE ®, Copyright © 1960, 1962, 1963, 1968, 1971, 1972, 1973,
1975, 1977, 1995 by The Lockman Foundation, Used by permission. (www.Lockman.org)

Verses marked "Amplified" are taken from THE AMPLIFIED BIBLE, Copyright © 1954, 1958,
1962, 1964, 1965, 1987 by the Lockman Foundation. All rights reserved. Used by permission. (www.
Lockman.org)

Verses marked "The Message" are taken from THE MESSAGE, Copyright © 1993, 1994, 1995,
1996, 2000, 2001, 2002. Used by permission of NavPress Publishing Group. (www.navpress.com)

Verses marked "NKJV" are taken from The New King James Bible, New Testament Copyright ©
1979 by Thomas Nelson, Inc. The New King James Bible, New Testament and Psalms Copyright ©
1980 by Thomas Nelson, Inc. (www.ThomasNelson.com)

Verses marked "NRSV" are taken from the NEW REVISED STANDARD VERSION BIBLE,
copyright © 1989 by the Division of Christian Education of the National Council of the Churches of
Christ in the U.S.A., and are used by permission. All rights reserved.

Verses marked "CEV" are taken from CONTEMPORARY ENGLISH VERSION, copyright ©
1995, American Bible Society. Used by permission.

Verses marked "JB" are taken from THE JERUSALEM BIBLE, copyright © 1966, 1967, and 1968 by
Darton, Longman & Todd Ltd and Doubleday & Company, Inc.

Verses marked "Moffatt" are taken from THE BIBLE: JAMES MOFFATT TRANSLATION,
copyright © 1922, 1924, 1925, 1926, 1935 by Harper Collins San Francisco. Copyright 1950, 1952,
1953, 1954 by James A. R. Moffatt.

Website:
www.HealingScienceToday.com

Printed in the United States of America.
ISBN: 978-1-4269-7010-8 (sc)
ISBN: 978-1-4269-7011-5 (e)

Trafford rev. 01/09/2012

www.trafford.com

North America & International
toll-free: 1 888 232 4444 (USA & Canada)
phone: 250 383 6864 ♦ fax: 812 355 4082

PREFACE

Marriage isn't for everyone, but a satisfying marriage isn't only for a select lucky few either. Although relationships have the same core values, a marriage is not the same as the relationships we have with friends, parents, or teachers. Marriage is a choice we make, to be involved in a unique relationship like no other. The reader will find in the book, *Marriage: Sink or Swim,* tips proven over time on how pro-actively to swim through a healthy marriage.

The booklet presents marriage as a moral safeguard and family building block, not as a human or religious duty. Partners can get along and work together profitably because spiritual unity is natural and can be nurtured.

Realistically, there is no human pat-answer to a healthy marriage because relationships are a work in progress open to increased knowledge and love. The ideas in *Marriage* expand on the knowledge of equal rights, empathy, and spirituality, synergizing with a progressive committed relationship.

Because a resilient foundation is requisite on which to build a solid partnership, other reading material has been inserted into this book. You will find a short article I wrote, *Calling Out the Naysayers,* along with the chapters: *Creation, Footsteps of Truth* and *Some Misconceptions Debunked.* The ideas in these chapters are from Mary Baker Eddy's *Science and Health*, an open-ended book aiding readers to discover their own inspired purpose and spiritual power. The ideas are based in divine Science.

Divine Science presents a countercosmology to the typical interpretation of creation as with a start and end. Creation has no beginning, no end. The reader of *Creation* is attracted to an ongoing revelation of Spirit and its formations, "In other words, matter is not a reality of being, but is an incorrect or undeveloped view of reality which disappears as Spirit comes into view."

Footsteps of Truth manages to explore birth, aging, diet, child-rearing, and dreaming from the framework of faith in a divine order.

The chapter, *Some Misconceptions Debunked,* serves as a reminder that the text on divine (Christian) Science is vulnerable to misinterpretation, as is any writing. Therefore the reader is encouraged to analyze and re-analyze whatever they read—even more, whatever they observe, feel, and experience in this indefinite world—so as to come to their own conclusions with divine Spirit.

Cheryl Petersen

CONTENTS

MARRIAGE/RELATIONSHIPS

No one should separate a couple that God has joined together.[1]

At the resurrection people will neither marry nor be given in marriage; but they will be like the angels in heaven.[2]

When Jesus came to John the Baptist for baptism, John was astounded and reluctant. Jesus read John's confused thoughts and reassured him with the remark, "Permit it at this time; for in this way it is fitting for us to fulfill all righteousness."[3] Apparently, Jesus acknowledged several human ceremonies as a means to advance spiritual good.

Marriage is the legal and moral provision for reproduction among humankind. Until spiritual reality is discerned intact and understood—as when John the Revelator[4] envisioned God's universe on earth where the temporal perceptions are replaced by spiritual perceptions—marriage will continue subject to policies that secure increasing virtue.

Fidelity to the marriage vow is required to preserve collective well-being in society. Infidelity is "the pestilence that stalks in the darkness . . . the plague that destroys at midday."[5] The instruction,

---

[1]   Matt. 19:6, Mark 10:9 (CEV)
[2]   Matt. 22:30; Luke 20:34-36
[3]   Matt. 3:15 (NASB)
[4]   Rev. 21:1
[5]   Ps. 91:6

"You shall not commit adultery,"[6] is no less imperative than, "You shall not murder."[7]

Abstinence from immoral sexual activity leads to an advanced state of intellectual, cultural, and material development in human society, marked by progress in the arts, science, and religion. Without integrity there is no social stability and one can't achieve the Science of Life.

Union of the masculine and feminine qualities *represents*, not *is,* completeness. The qualities, regarded as feminine or masculine, reach a higher tone through a blending of certain elements such as courage, strength, or empathy. The harmony of spiritual oneness is felt as the differing elements join naturally with each other. All persons, regardless of gender, should be forgiving, chaste, tender, and strong. The attraction between these spiritual qualities will be perpetual only as they are pure and true, being constantly renewed like the returning springtime.

The religious practice of marriage has declined, especially in the European countries; however the moral practice of forming a monogamous union with both parents at home raising the children shows faithfulness can support a healthy partnership and family.

The demands of the affections will never be satisfied if you pursue a sexy, rich, or sanctimonious partner, so make sure to engage with wisdom, sincerity, and open-mindedness. Spiritual happiness lasts because it is constantly poured forth from Truth and Love. Genuine happiness can't exist alone, because it has to be shared.

It may seem vain to share our love with someone who doesn't give it back, but it isn't a waste as long as we allow spiritual Love to enlarge, purify, and elevate the circumstance. If spite, close-mindedness, and arrogance do uproot and scatter our affections, this separation of fleshly ties serves to unite thought more closely to God, for Love supports the struggling heart until it ceases to sigh over the world and recognizes the spiritual cosmos.

---

6   Ex. 20:14; Deut. 5:18; Matt. 5:27
7   Ex. 20:13; Deut. 5:17

Marriage is fortunate or unfortunate according to the expectations it involves and fulfills. A promising motive in any relationship is to participate in activities adapted to improve society. Unity of spirit gives new energy to a sense of joy, whereas lame or unreasonable expectations drag joy through the mud.

Musical notes can be arranged to make harmony, or noise. Tones of the human mind are just as diverse as musical notes, and harmony is apparent as tones of unselfish ambition, noble life-motives, and honesty blend properly. Spiritual harmony constitutes individual and collective happiness, strength, and permanence.

Spiritual and moral freedom is found in Soul. Guard against narrowness and jealousy which confine a wife or husband to restricted behavior. Home is not a boundary of the affections, but is a framework from which to grow spiritually. It is beneficial never to want all the attention and time of your partner. Circulate happiness and compassion in the community to promote the sweet interchange of confidence and love, but be sure not to generate a wandering desire for incessant amusement outside the home circle.

In his book, *Survival in the Killing Fields*,[8] Haing Ngor, survivor of the Khmer Rouge regime, acknowledges the special trust between he and his wife, which did not include quibbling. Having money and possessions may remove some barriers to a happy marriage, but nothing can replace the loving care in a union. Hard feelings are avoided when spouses use common sense, have respect for one another, and do not become extravagant or lazy.

Fully recognize your ongoing responsibilities before entering matrimony. "A married woman is concerned . . . how she can please her husband,"[9] says the Bible. Success is guaranteed when both spouses are pleasant. Have a mindful interest in one another's progress and happily reciprocate appreciation in a relationship.

Mutual compromises or a prenuptial agreement will often preserve an arrangement which might otherwise become unbearable. Agree on a realistic intent of the marriage and share the responsibilities to meet that intent. As you both fulfill the different demands of your united

---

[8] Haing Ngor, with Roger Warner, *Survival in the Killing Fields.* (New York, NY: Carroll & Graf Publishers, 2003)

[9] I Cor. 7:34

spheres, you will feel supported, confident, and thus sanctify the union of wellbeing in which the heart finds peace and home.

Gentle words, and an unselfish attention to detail in what promotes the success of your spouse, will prove valuable in prolonging one another's health and smiles rather than stolid indifference or resentment. Remember, a simple heartfelt word or deed is powerful enough to renew the romance.

It is silly to complain about incompatibility. Do not deceive yourself, or one another, as to why you are getting married or staying married. Deception is fatal to happiness. Either before or after the legal union, you can understand a sensible motive for marriage.

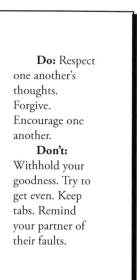

Do: Respect one another's thoughts. Forgive. Encourage one another. **Don't:** Withhold your goodness. Try to get even. Keep tabs. Remind your partner of their faults.

The frequency of divorce shows that the sacredness of this relationship is losing its influence, and that serious mistakes are undermining the foundation of marriage. Separation need not take place if both husband and wife genuinely put into practice spiritual rules of Truth and Love. Spiritual knowledge inevitably lifts one's being higher in the scale of harmony and happiness. When the moral obligations are kept intact, why annul the nuptial vow?

Similar tastes, intents, and aspirations are necessary to form a loving and permanent companionship. The beautiful in character is also the good, welding indissolubly the links of affection. From the logic of events we learn that selfishness and impurity are short-lived and that wisdom will ultimately separate what she did not join together.

The parent's affection cannot be weaned from their children, because parent-love includes purity and constancy, both of which are immortal. Paternal care lives on under all situations.

Marriage should improve the human species, becoming a barrier against stupidity, a protection and encouragement to the spouses, and a nucleus for the expressed feelings. However, in a majority of cases, marriage is used to blame or control, because human beings neglect their spiritual growth and spend time and thought living in the past, pursuing superficial goals, trying to prove the other wrong, or showing off.

A badly trained ear calls noisy melodrama normal, not appreciating harmony. So, human perception, untrained to discern the true happiness of being, misunderstands the source of happiness. Divine Science will correct the misunderstandings and teach us life's sweeter harmonies.

> Couples who use one another to show off or get attention could end up bickering.

Soul has infinite resources with which to bless humankind, and happiness is more readily responded to and more secure in our keeping, if found in Soul. Higher enjoyments alone can satisfy the cravings of immortal person. Happiness can't be defined by personal perceptions. The perceptions of human beings confer no lasting enjoyment.

Happiness is won as the good has ascendency over the evil and the spiritual over the animal. The attainment of this spiritual condition improves our progeny, diminishes crime, and gives higher aims to ambition. Every valley of materialism must be exalted and every mountain of selfishness must be brought low, that the highway of our God may be prepared in Science. The offspring of heavenly-minded parents inherit more intellect, better balanced minds, and a more reliable health.

If some unfortunate circumstance places promising children in the arms of gross parents, often these beautiful children wither like tropical flowers born in the snowy Alps. If by chance those children live to become parents themselves, they may reproduce in their own helpless children the grosser traits of what they were taught when young. Society can ask: What hope of happiness, what noble ambition can inspire the child who inherits propensities that must be overcome before reducing the child to a wreck?

Raising children is a great responsibility, a more solemn trust than climbing the corporate ladder or accumulating material possessions. Take immense care not to transmit to children what is unworthy of perpetuity.

In order to advance humankind, the development of mortals must improve. The scientific mental spirit of marriage is unity. Having sex is acceptable for the purpose of reproducing a higher human species. Every stage of child-bearing must be kept mentally pure and have the sanctity of virginity.

Educate the children to form habits agreeable to moral and spiritual law. Then the children are better prepared to meet and master the limitations imposed by physical laws, especially the laws that breed disease and disorder.

Parents, if you allow your children incessantly to play computer games, want stuff, or be picky, don't complain later in life if your children are complicated or frivolous. Children should be allowed to keep their innocence and yet mature through growth in the understanding of man and woman's higher nature. If you worry less "about your life, what you will eat or drink; or about your body, what you will wear,"[10] you will do more for the wellbeing of children than you can imagine.

Conscientious parenting includes fostering discipline, industriousness and respect.

By attributing more and more intelligence to spirituality, and giving less power to physical laws and human beings, we promote wisdom and health. The divine Mind, which forms the bud and blossom, will care for the human body, even as it clothes the lily.[11] Do not let mortals interfere with God's natural order of existence by thrusting in laws of mistaken, human perceptions.

Bear in mind, the higher nature of a person is really not controlled by the lower more baneful nature; if it were the order of wisdom would be reversed. Our immature views of life hide eternal harmony and produce the problems of which we complain. Even though human beings believe in mortal laws, which by default cause people to disbelieve the Science of Mind, this does not make the materialist view first and the superior law of Soul last. You would not think food supplements were better for warding off disease than the influential Mind if you understood the Science of being.

---

[10] Matt. 6:25, 31; Luke 12:29
[11] Matt. 6:28; Luke 12:27

In spiritual knowledge, we are the offspring of Spirit, Mind. The beautiful, good, and uncorrupt constitute our ancestry. Our origin is not like that of mortals, programmed, nor do we pass through humanly determined stages prior to reaching intelligence. Spirit is our primordial and ultimate source of being. God is our Father-Mother, and Life is the law of our being.

Civil laws are implementing fairness and equity between the rights of the sexes, but more progress is needed, to say the least. Civilization and Science stand strong on the side of justice and encourage the elimination of discrimination, however, every time an effort is made to remedy unfairness, we must be alert that the effort doesn't encourage difficulties of greater magnitude. Higher aims and motives, as well as improved mental character, must be considered as the feasible and rational means of progress.

If a spouse deserts the partnership, certainly the lone mate can single-handedly be self-reliant and independent. Women and men are equally capable to succeed in the business world, earn an education, own real estate, and care for the children and home, without interference.

Global injustice between the sexes is a crying evil caused by the arrogance and inhumanity of mortals. We must exercise our faith in the direction taught by the Apostle James, when he said: "Religion that God and Father accepts as pure and faultless is this: to look after orphans and widows in their distress and to keep oneself from being polluted by the world."[12]

Husbands and wives, who keep empathy and generosity to themselves, will become tyrants. Primitive Christianity includes humanitarian efforts to help people who are less fortunate. We can assist others without becoming unfaithful to our partner. Do not let selfishness, suspicion, or bitterness control one another's activities.

A solid marriage is one that signifies a union of hearts. Furthermore, the time comes when Jesus declared that in the resurrection "people will neither marry nor be given in marriage; but they will be like the angels in heaven."[13] Marriage won't lose its luster as the love/hate emotion gives way to the rejoicing of Soul. Recognize your ability to

---

[12]   James 1:27
[13]   Matt. 22:30

unite masculine and feminine insight, love, spiritual understanding, and perpetual peace.

Until it is learned that God is Father-Mother, marriage will be useful as long as mortals do not permit an unlawfulness that leads to a worse state of society than now exists. Sincerity and uprightness ensure the stability of the marriage promise. Physical mortals ultimately claim nothing in the end, and Spirit receives its own.

Learn from experience. Learn respect, self-control, patience, and a reliable happiness that comes from spiritual growth. May Christ, Truth, be present at every bridal altar, to turn the water into wine[14] and inspire your life with discernment of a serene and immortal existence.

> When a partner points out a bad habit, don't justify or defend the bad habit. Don't crack a sarcastic joke about it. Be quiet. Listen. Learn. Act. Exchange the bad habit for a good one.

If the starting point of your relationship is consistent with progress, it will be strong and enduring. However, the union of the sexes suffers fearful conflict. Divorces warn us that some fundamental error lingers in marriage. To achieve divine Science and its harmony, it pays to regard life more metaphysically.

Evil is conspicuously broadcast today, showing off itself in materialism and sensualism, but looking closer, we notice they are struggling against the advancing spiritual era. The world may lack spirituality, and people may not be able to keep a promise or make a home happy, but human minds are demanding an improved attitude.

As with any reform, a transition period will be felt. Transition periods are often not pleasant, but are unsettling and undesirable; however, why buck the trend when we are compelled to find permanence and peace in a more spiritual devotion?

The mental development that has brought infidelity to the surface will continue to fight for improvement in order to strengthen marriage.

---

[14] John 2:9

Rick Warren wrote in *The Purpose Drive Life,* "Your most profound and intimate experiences of worship will likely be in your darkest days—when your heart is broken, when you feel abandoned, when you're out of options, when the pain is great—and you turn to God alone."[15]

Adversity teaches human beings not to lean on a collapsible crutch. Sorrow can be therapeutic, forcing us to enter the domain of spiritual happiness and reliance. We don't remember this when life is fine. But when mortals belch or the economy goes sour or people think their partner is boring, undoubtedly the heart is pierced with sadness. Spiritual development, however, doesn't come from planting seeds in the dirt of materialist views. Those seeds rot whereas Love nurtures the higher joys of Spirit, which have no taint of earth. God will take care of us as we develop spiritually on a trajectory unfolding new views of divine goodness and love.

When a relationship is going well, pay attention, otherwise an increasing dependence on one another may yank the rug out from under your feet. If, on the other hand, your relationship is rocky, don't react, but hope, pray, and wait patiently on divine wisdom to point the way.

Husbands and wives should never separate if there is no Christian demand for it. The logic of events will reveal itself. In those cases when one spouse is better than the other, than the better spouse is

> "When God asks someone to do something for Him entailing sacrifice, He makes up for it in surprising ways. God has not let me down. Though He had led Bill all over the world to preach the gospel, He had not forgotten the little family in the mountains of North Carolina. I have watched with gratitude as God has guided each child."
>
> Ruth Bell Graham, wife of international evangelist, Billy Graham. From the book, *Ruth: A Portrait,* by Patricia Cornwell

---

[15]   Warren, Rick. *The Purpose Driven Life.* Michigan: Zondervan, 2002. www.zondervan.com

good company for the worse. Dr. Oral Roberts discusses his philosophy for a successful marriage. He and his wife, Evelyn, who was better company for a time, patiently told her very busy husband that he was "making a terrible mistake,"[16] by neglecting the family. Her words struck Mr. Robert's conscience and he disciplined himself to put God and family first before work

> Thank your partner daily, not to get your way, but to be truly thankful for their expression of spiritual goodness.

Unhappiness has a reward when our outlook is expanded and purified. It is life-giving to learn the lessons God teaches. The furnace separates the gold from the dross that the precious metal may be graven with the image of God.

When navigating aircraft through a storm, the pressure is shifting, the wind is shrieking, and air pockets are hiding in the air currents. We ask the pilot: "Do you know your course? Can you aviate safely among this turbulence?" Though brave, the dauntless aviator is not sure of safety because even aeronautical science is not equal to the Science of Mind. Yet, acting on his or her highest understanding, the pilot doesn't avoid responsibility, but keeps working, ready to act on divine guidance. This example of behavior can be useful in any stressful relationship, including a seething marriage. Be accountable, hope and work, willingly act on divine guidance, not private interest. Divine guidance will either force a graceful change, or calm the enraged atmosphere.

To assume an alpha male or female attitude adds to one's character is absurd. Through spiritual ascendency our Lord and Master healed the sick, raised the dead, and commanded even the winds and waves to obey him. Grace and Truth are potent beyond all other means and methods.

The lack of spiritual power in today's demonstrations of popular Christianity does not put to silence the labor of the centuries. Spiritual, not a materialist consciousness is needed. Men and women, delivered

---

16   Roberts, Oral. *When You See the Invisible You Can Do the Impossible.* Copyright 2002, used by permission of Destiny Image Publishers, 167 Walnut Bottom Road. Shippensburg, PA 17257 www. destinyimage.com

from conflict, disease, and death will epitomize the true likeness of God's image.

Religious and medical systems treat physical pains and pleasures as if they are normal, but Jesus rebuked the suffering from any such cause or effect. The epoch approaches when true religion will be built on the understanding of the truth of being. However, people are slow to understand truth because they are obsessed with fashion, pride, bodies, and opinion. The fixation of materiality makes us tired because it goes against our higher nature. At some point, we will pierce through the fleeting and false and learn how Spirit, the great architect, has created men and women in Science.

> Obsessions of any kind blind a person to progressive decisions.

Envy buries trust and love. Mistrust is a rotten apple in a relationship. Build a confidence in the commitment and responsibility that comes with a union. Don't rush into a relationship teetering on infatuation or fear. Be aware of how your promises will influence your own growth and other people's lives.

I discredit the belief that asexual propagation applies to the human species.

Spiritual Science presents unfoldment, not accumulation; revelation, not big bang. There is no growth from material molecule to mind. Creation is a manifest impartation of divine Mind to man and woman and the universe. As human generation ceases, the unbroken links of eternal harmonious being will be discerned; and person, not of

> Be alert: If a person is angry at their partner or child, that anger spreads out in the world. So, nurture honesty and love. When we love, love is shared and felt.

the mortal flesh, but coexistent with God, will appear. The scientific fact that man and woman and the universe are evolved from Spirit, and so are spiritual, is as fixed in divine Science as is the proof that mortals gain the experience of health only as they lose the sense of destruction and disease. Mortals can never understand God's creation while believing that human beings are creators. Whether marriage or reproduction happen or not, God's children, spiritual beings, already created, will be recognized as we awake to the truth of being. Spiritually to understand that there is but one creator, God, reveals all creation, confirms Scripture, brings the sweet assurance of no parting, no pain, which in turn exposes deathless, perfect, and eternal person.

When practicing Christian Science and educating your own offspring spiritually, know that you can educate others spiritually and not conflict with the scientific sense of God's creation. One day, a child will ask, "Do you keep the First Commandment? Do you have one God and creator, or are human beings creators?" If you answer, "God creates human beings through human beings," the child may retort, "Do you teach that Spirit creates materially, or do you teach that Spirit is infinite; therefore all limited material perceptions are out of the question?" Jesus said, "The people of this age marry and are given in marriage. But those who are considered worthy of taking part in that age and in the resurrection from the dead will neither marry nor be given in marriage."[17]

---

[17] Matt. 22:30; Mark 12:25; Luke 20:34-35

CREATION

Your throne was established long ago; you are from all eternity.[18]

We know that the whole creation has been groaning as in the pains of childbirth right up to the present time. Not only so, but we ourselves, who have the firstfruits of the Spirit, groan inwardly as we wait eagerly for our adoption, the redemption of our bodies.[19]

Eternal Truth is changing the universe, and physical forces are trying to keep up. Don't be impressed by materialist views, but instead, experience spiritual thought expanding into expression. "Let there be light,"[20] is the perpetual demand of Truth and Love, changing chaos into order and discord into the music of the spheres.[21] The mythical and scholarly theories of creation provide nothing to build on and are a far cry from views of creation as revealed by infinite Mind.

Human beings habitually belittle divine Mind with immature perceptions of cause and effect. The restricted perceptions, juxtaposed with physical sense testimony, confuse creation with speculation. The materialist view, always looking for a first cause, can't explain or contain

> Learn something new and genuine each day.

---

18   Ps. 93:2
19   Rom. 8:22-23 (TNIV)
20   Gen. 1:3
21   Music of the spheres is a concept frequently credited to Greek philosopher Pythagoras (569 B.C.-approximately 500 B.C.

God and furthermore can't explain the one cause and effect with no beginning, no end.

The human or physical structure can't be made the basis of any true idea of infinite God. Physical eyes and ears have not seen or heard Spirit.

Advancing to a higher level of activity, consciousness pierces the materialist view and discovers the spiritual view. Progress removes the restraints that physical senses impose on human beings, and the finite yields to the infinite. Thought shakes off the scholastic and mortal and moves toward the inspirational and immortal. All things are created spiritually. Mind, not matter, is the creator. Love, the divine Principle, is the Father-Mother of the universe, including person.

The theology of the Trinity points to one undivided, "Hear, O Israel: The Lord our God, the Lord is one"[22] The Trinity is not three persons in one, suggesting polytheism or multiple personalities, but is existence based on the one ever-present I AM.

> The Trinity is not meant to be confusing. It isn't an obstacle between you and God, Love.

The everlasting I AM is not bounded or compressed within the narrow limits of physical humanity, nor can Spirit be correctly understood through mortal concepts. The precise form of God is not very important. Ask rather; What is infinite Mind or divine Love?

Who is it that requires our obedience? God, who "controls the stars in the sky and everyone on this earth. When God does something, we cannot change it or even ask why."[23]

No form or physical organization can adequately represent Love. A materialist sense of God leads to narrow-mindedness and regimented behavior; it restricts the essence of spirituality.

A limitless Mind will not be known through a limited human mind. Finiteness can't present the idea or the vastness of infinity. A mind which came from a limited source will be limited, whereas a mind that comes from infinite Mind will reveal an infinite emanation, a scientific creation. Mind is all.

---

[22] Deut. 6:4
[23] Dan. 4:35 (CEV)

Is matter or Spirit substance? The theory that Spirit is not the only real substance is pantheistic heterodoxy to the people who worship Spirit. The belief that matter and spirit are a mixture leads to sickness, sin, and death. Measurable particles and waves produce measurable outcomes, but Spirit is immeasurable.

Mind creates the likeness of ideas, and the substance of an idea is polar opposite to the substance of non-intelligent matter. God did not create a physical universe as described through a materialist view. Materialist views confuse spiritual ideas with human conceptions and lean toward anthropomorphism. God is not anthropomorphic, but is divine Principle—in other words, divine Love—and brings "forth the constellations in their seasons,"[24] and leads "out the Bear with its cubs."[25]

> God did not create human beings, money, physical locations, and mortal jobs. God reveals sincerity, balance, grandness, joy, purpose, and spiritual identities.

A limited mind manifests all sorts of anomalies, and causes the mind-in-matter theory to be seen as conflictive. No one has found temporal mind, life, or love sufficient to satisfy the demands of human lack and anguish. Our desires and aspirations ache to be fulfilled and a reward is felt when we stop limiting infinite Mind to finite resources. Infinite Mind can't lose its character as inexhaustible Love, eternal Life, omnipotent Truth.

It would require an infinite form to contain infinite Mind, indeed the phrase *infinite form* is an oxymoron. Finite human beings cannot be the image and likeness of the infinite God. A mortal or finite conception of God cannot embrace the glories of limitless, bodiless Life and Love. Finiteness causes mortals to crave something better, higher, and holier than what the human mind comes up with concerning a physical creator and creation. Spiritual views supply the true idea, which in turn prove the insufficiency and falsity of materialist views.

---

[24]   Job 38:32
[25]   *ibid*

People are more than a material shell with a mind stuck inside. Spirituality is more than a soul trying to escape a human experience in order to be immortal. We reflect infinity, and this reflection is the true idea of God.

Spiritual selfhood is infinitely being expressed, broadening and ascending from a boundless basis. Mind manifests all that exists in the infinitude of Truth. The only way we will know our true divine image and likeness, is to know God properly.

The infinite Principle is reflected by the infinite idea and spiritual individuality, but the human ego and physical senses have no cognizance of either Principle or its idea. As human beings gain the true perception of people and God, the human abilities are refined and sharpened.

Mortals have an imperfect understanding of spiritual being and its infinite range of thought. Eternal Life belongs to spiritual being. Never born and never dying, it is impossible for people under the government of God in eternal Science to fall from an immortal status.

> Practice using spiritual sense—a sense of divine Spirit—and this helps to know God better.

Through spiritual perception we can discern the heart of divinity and thereby begin to understand the generic term *person* in Science. Our spirituality is not absorbed in God. We do not become isolated or trapped in a vacuum. Our individuality goes on and on reflecting Life eternal. We each represent the totality of infinite Mind's substance.

In divine Science, person is the true image of God. The divine nature was skillfully personified by Christ Jesus, who shed light on a powerful concept of God, and even shifted the people's thought to experience something better than what they had been trained to think was normal. Jesus served to remove the stereotypical view of people as sinners destined to be sick and dying. The Christlike understanding of scientific being and divine healing includes a perfect Principle and idea—complete God and complete person—as the basis of thought and demonstration.

If person was once complete or perfect, but then lost his/her perfection, then the image of God was never known. The *lost* image is not an image. The true likeness can't be lost in divine reflection. Understanding this, Jesus said: "You shall be perfect, just as your Father in heaven is perfect."[26]

Human perceptions transmit their own images and form offspring after human illusions; whereas God, Spirit, works spiritually, not materially. Brain is an electrical device unable to originate a human concept, because electricity has no intelligence, no creative ability. Immortal ideas—pure, perfect, and enduring—are transmitted by the divine Mind through Science and demands spiritual thoughts to the end that they may produce harmonious results.

> Our views of God and people change. Be open to views connected to forgiveness. Have the spiritual courage to change your life habits to help the masses and not just a select few people.

The study of divine Science helps eliminate a faulty thought process. Reasoning that begins with imperfection will end with imperfection. Reasoning that begins with perfection will arrive at perfection. A sculptor can't perfect her outlines while concentrating on an imperfect model. The painter can't depict the features and appearance of Jesus while thinking about the character of Judas Iscariot.

The perceptions and realities of mortal thought either die or give way to the spiritual discovery of completeness and eternity. Through many generations, human beliefs reach diviner conceptions and the immortal model of God's revelation is finally seen as the only true conception of being.

Science not only reveals reasonable possibilities but also prompts human beings to discover what God has already done. You must trust your ability to experience goodness and to bring out better and higher results. Don't become a sluggard. Be alert so as to save yourself from the possibility of failure.

A sick body evolves from sick thoughts. Illness, disease, and death proceed from fear. Debauchery causes hurtful physical and moral conditions.

---

[26]   Matt. 5:48 (NKJV)

Promiscuousness and self-centeredness are educated in mortal mind when humans repeat the same thoughts over and over, or when they constantly talk about the body or expect pleasure or pain from the body. This exercise pushes away spiritual growth. Don't be surprised, when wrapping yourself up in mortal thinking, you will lose out wearing your immortal nature.

When we expect pleasure from the body, we get pain. When we look for life in the body, we find death. When we search for Truth or Spirit in material things, we find uncertainty. Now reverse this process. Look away from matter into Truth and Love, the Principle of all happiness, harmony, and immortality. Let your thought embrace the enduring, the honest, and the genuine, and you will bring these into your experience according to how often they occupy your thoughts. We are learning that the human mind affects our health and happiness.

> It requires spiritual ambition to un-learn thoughts and behavior that do not lead us to modesty and stability.

There are innumerable accounts of people becoming preoccupied and naturally forgetting their body and its complaints. Our attention can be so focused on reaching a spiritual goal that pain is forgotten and shown to be powerless in the presence of good works. For example, after the September 11th, 2001 plane attacks on the Twin Towers in New York City, many people, especially firefighters performed miraculous feats saving lives, oblivious to their own bodies.

Detach feelings from the body, or matter, which is only a type of human belief, and learn the meaning of God, or good, and the nature of the immutable and immortal. Don't worry when breaking away from mutating time and feelings, because you will not lose a sense of reality, life, or your own identity. As you contemplate spiritual reality, consciousness is purified and being groomed to experience the celestial; similar to a chick which has broken from the shell and preened its wings for a skyward flight.

We can forget the body while remembering good and the human race. Good compels us to solve the problem of being. Commitment to good increases our dependence on a spiritual God and shows a paramount necessity to be responsible to Truth and Love. Christian

Science does not claim the perfection of God, but ascribes to God the entire glory. By taking "off your old self with its practices,"[27] mortals are clothed "with immortality."[28]

Humans can't figure out the nature and quality of God's creation by diving into shallow materialist beliefs. The efforts to find life and truth in matter is tentative, therefore we must improve the effort and pay attention to spiritual sense and an immortal idea of substance. Spiritual, clearer, higher views inspire the Godlike person to reach the absolute center and circumference of reality.

Job said: "My ears had heard of you but now my eyes have seen you."[29] Humans will echo Job's thought when the pain and pleasure of material bodies cease to predominate. People can learn to distinguish between fake happiness and true. We can feel the pleasure of loving unselfishly, working patiently, and conquering all that is unlike God as we highly value spiritual perceptions. "For where your treasure is, there your heart will be also."[30]

Where does the cacophony of life come from? Disorder comes when matter is considered to be a cause. Matter is not a cause or effect. Divine Mind is the only cause or Principle of existence. Your thought process, or mental treatment must begin with divine Mind, not the brain, not human mind, not physical form.

Human beings are egotists. They stroll around believing themselves to be independent workers, elite authors, or privileged originators of something God could in no way ever manifest. The creations of human mind represent the foibles of existence whereas spiritual people represent the truth of creation.

When human beings blend their thoughts of existence with the spiritual and work only as Truth and Love works, they will taste heaven and stop groping in the dark and clinging to the world. In his book, *The Power of Now,* Eckhart Tolle says, "You can still be active and enjoy manifesting and

> Respect goes to those great athletes, leaders, parents, teachers, and so on, who are outstanding at what they do, to glorify God.

---

27   Col. 3:9
28   I Cor. 15:53
29   Job 42:5
30   Matt. 6:21; Luke 12:34

creating new forms, and circumstances, but you won't be identified with them. You do not need them to give you a sense of self. They are not your life—only your life situation."[31] It is important to remember to stay out of the dark beliefs that cheat us and make us involuntary hypocrites. Don't be induced to believe you are doing good when really you are producing evil, injuring others, and deforming goodness. People who think they are a semi-god will mis-create. In Bible language: "I cannot be good as I desire to be, and I do wrong against my wishes."[32]

There can be but one creator, who has created all. Whatever seems to be a new creation is only the discovery of some distant idea of Truth; or else it is a self-division of mortal thought. The human mind is not an originator, but is a mime, attempting to mimic the divine infinite.

The multiplication of humans is neither creation nor revelation, but is the human mind's misrepresentation of scientific eternal consciousness of creation.

The relativity of matter, the complex human body, and the turbulent earth are fleeting concepts of humans, trained to believe life is mortal. Fleeting concepts have their day before the permanent facts and their completeness in Spirit appear. The complicated creations of human thought must finally give place to the glorious forms which we sometimes glimpse through the eye of divine Mind when the mental picture is spiritual and eternal. Take the time to look past the fading, sensational pictures and gain the true sense of life. Rest your gaze on the unsearchable realm of Mind. Look ahead and act as possessing all power from Truth and Love in whom you have your being.

As humanity expands their correct views of God and people, countless objects of creation, which you did not see before, will be seen. When you realize that Life is Spirit, never in nor of matter, this

> Once it is realized that the human mind creates its own circumstances, the next step is to push past the unreliable, limited human mind and seek God, infinite Mind. In God, things really happen and they are good.

---

31   *The Power of Now: A Guide to Spiritual Enlightenment* Copyright 1999 by Eckhart Tolle. Reprinted with permission of New World Library, Novato, CA www.NewWorldLibrary.com

32   Rom. 7:19 (Moffatt)

understanding will develop into self-completeness, finding all in God, good, and needing no other consciousness.

What are the realities of being? Spirit and its formations. In other words, matter is not a reality of being, but is an incorrect or undeveloped view of reality which disappears as Spirit comes into view. Sin, sickness and death were unseen by Jesus, proving the view of Spirit to be truthful. We recognize and feel the true existence and unspeakable peace as we give evidence of spiritual living and inviolability. Peace comes from an all-embracing spiritual love.

The approach of Christian Science is to recognize the spiritual identity of people and to see and understand God's creation—all the glories of earth and heaven and its inhabitants.

The universe of Spirit is peopled with spiritual beings, and its government is divine Science. Man and woman are the offspring of the highest qualities of Mind. We understand spiritual existence in proportion to our understanding of Truth and Love. Humans must gravitate Godward. Humans will become more humane as their desires and aims grow spiritual. As sin and mortality are discarded, human beings catch the broader interpretations of being and secure a lasting sense of the infinite.

This scientific sense of being, turning from matter to Spirit, by no means suggests we are absorbed into Deity or that we lose our identity. A scientific sense of being reveals a clearer distinct individuality, a wider sphere of thought and action, a more expansive inclusive love, and a more permanent peace.

> If our spiritual journey does make us self-absorbed or isolated chances are we took a wrong turn.

Mortal birth and death comes across as irresistible or untimely, however God's people aren't mortals. Mortals are unreal and obsolete. The truth of being is perennial. We are God's image and likeness.

When we feel the loss of human peace, the desire for spiritual joy gets stronger. This desire for heavenly good comes even before we discover what belongs to wisdom and Love. The loss of earthly hopes and pleasures can brighten the spiritual path. Pain in the body informs us that pleasure in the body is mortal, compelling us to discover spiritual joy.

The pains of the body can be salutary, if they force the mind to dig itself out of false beliefs and transplant its affections in Soul, where the creations of God are good, "giving joy to the heart."[33] The sword of Science decapitates error with Truth. Materiality gives place to our higher individuality and destiny.

> Don't become overly passionate by the earthly losses (or gains) because God sent heavenly good.

Would life without friends be empty? Then the time will come when you will feel alone, without sympathy, but this vacuum is filled with divine Love. When this time comes, even if you cling to a sense of personal joys, spiritual Love will force you to accept what best promotes your spiritual growth. Friends will betray and enemies will slander, until the lesson is learned, and you are exalted; for "man's extremity is God's opportunity."[34] I speak from experience. We are learning to lay down our fleshliness and gain spirituality by ridding our self of a mortal identity. Universal Love is the divine way in Christian Science.

Wrongdoers make their own hell by doing things which avoid Life, Truth, and Love. Saints make their own heaven by embracing Life, Truth, and Love. Wrongdoers believe they are happier when being negative, but this is evil aiding evil. Do not be deceived by inverted human conclusions.

Following Jesus' sayings and demonstrations helps us overcome the flesh. The base and narrow beliefs which originate in mortals are hell. Spiritual person is the idea of Spirit, reflecting the presence of virtue and illuming the universe with light. Spirituality is deathless, above sin or frailty. We do not cross over into the vast forever of Life, but we coexist with God and the universe. Complete and infinite Mind ordained is heaven.

The objects of material thinking will be destroyed while the spiritual idea, whose substance is in Mind, is eternal. The offspring of God don't start from dust or a material cell. The offspring of God are in and of Spirit, divine Mind, and so forever continue. God is one. The

---

33   Ps. 19:8
34   Quote attributed to John Flavel, (1627-1691) English Presbyterian.

allness of Deity is God's oneness. Generically, person is one, meaning all people.

It is generally agreed upon that God is Father, eternal, self-created, infinite. If this is true, the forever Father must have had children prior to Adam. There is no linear life cycle that begins with Adam. We coexist with God. The great, I WILL BE WHAT I WILL BE[35] made all "that has been made."[36]

The Bible has Jesus saying, "For whoever does the will of my Father in heaven is my brother and sister and mother."[37] In a religious sense, the common name of mother, brother, and sister is identified with those doing God's will.

When examined in the light of divine Science, we see past the surface of mortals and detect inverted thoughts and erroneous beliefs and learn not to be fooled by them. Or, in a circuitous manner, we borrow thought from a higher source than matter and reverse the errors, to see celestial Truth replace error. Clothed in Spirit, appearance is "bright as a flash of lightning"[38]—like the garment of Christ. Even in this world, therefore, "always be clothed in white."[39] "Anyone who meets a testing challenge head-on and manages to stick it out is mighty fortunate. For such persons loyally in love with God, the reward is life and more life."[40]

---

[35]   Ex. 3:14
[36]   John 1:3
[37]   Matt. 12:50; Mark 3:35; Luke 8:23
[38]   Luke 9:29
[39]   Eccl. 9:8
[40]   James 1:12 (*The Message*)

FOOTSTEPS OF TRUTH

> Remember, Lord, how your servant has been mocked, how I bear in my heart the taunts of all the nations, the taunts with which your enemies have mocked, O Lord, with which they have mocked every step of your anointed one.[41]

The best sermon ever preached is the practice and manifestation of Truth, with replaces sickness, sin, and death. Jesus was quoted to have said, "You can't worship two gods at once."[42] We can ask our self, What one ideal am I committed to? We can't devote our self to more than one ideal.

It is not safe to build on false foundations. Truth makes a new creature, where "old things passed away; behold, new things have come."[43] Obsessions, selfishness, misleading appetites, hatred, fear, and lust give way to spirituality, and the superabundance of being is on the side of God, good.

We cannot fill vessels already full. Vessels full of the impracticable must first be emptied. Let us strip off error and stand in the showers of God and come clean.

The way to extract error from human mind is to pour in truth through flood-waters of Love. Spiritual perfection, including Christian perfection, is won on no other basis.

---

[41] Ps. 89:50-51
[42] Matt. 6:24; Luke 16:13 (The Message)
[43] II Cor. 5:17 (NASB)

Grafting spirituality on something not spiritual is as foolish as trying to "strain out a gnat" and "swallow a camel!"[44] Sin needs to be abandoned before forgiven.

The scientific relationship which exists between us and God must be worked out in life-practice. The will of God must universally be done.

As we shift our faith and attention from the pains and pleasures of temporal sense to the study of the Science of divine Mind, we get better instead of worse. Suffering, imprisonment, and death are not natural disciplinarians. The whole human family can be redeemed through the excellence of Christ—through the perception and acceptance of Truth. For this magnificent result Christian Science lights the torch of spiritual understanding.

Outside of divine Science all is relative. Earthly experience exposes the relativity of error, indirectly leading to the infinite capacities of Truth. Spiritual beings agree with the absolute and harmonious Principle of being. Immortality does not sin, suffer, or die and our spiritual experiences will multiply instead of diminish as God's kingdom comes on earth. The spiritual way leads to Life instead of to death and we realize our God-given dominion to overcome temporal limitations.

The thinking that God is all-power contradicts the practice of giving power to drugs or the human mind. Error abounds where Truth should "much more abound."[45] We admit that God has almighty power and is "an ever-present help in trouble,"[46] and yet we rely on drugs and the power of suggestion to heal disease and bad habits. Senseless matter or erring human mind has no power because omnipotent Spirit has all power.

Common opinion admits that a human being may catch a cold in the act of doing a good deed. Some people even fear and expect that the cold will develop into a fatal pulmonary disease. Evil cannot overpower the law of Love and stop the reward for doing good deeds. In the Science of spirituality, Mind—omnipotence—has all-power. Divine Mind, God assigns sure rewards to spiritual righteousness and shows that matter cannot heal or make sick, create or destroy.

---

[44] Matt. 23:24
[45] Rom. 5:20 (KJV)
[46] Ps. 46:1

If God were understood instead of only believed, this understanding would establish health. The church leaders of old accused Jesus, "because he claimed to be the Son of God."[47] The accusation was really the justification of Jesus, for to the Christ-like follower, the only true spirit is Godlike. The godly thought impels a more exalted worship and self-discipline. Spiritual perception brings out the possibilities of being and destroys reliance on anything accept God. Action and thought were made to image forth our Maker.

We are susceptible to believe in either more than one supreme Ruler, or in some power less than God. We imagine that Mind can be stuck in a sensuous body. What happens when the material body takes a turn for the worse and gives out? What happens when evil overloads the belief of life in matter and crashes? Human beings will believe that the deathless Principle, or Soul, escapes from matter and lives on; however, this is not true. Death is not a springboard to eternal Life and happiness. The so-called sinner, or person who neglects their spirituality, is a suicide. Sin kills the sinner and will continue to kill so long as the sin is committed. The ranting and raving of illegitimate living and of fearful and pitiful dying should disappear on the shore of time where the waves of sin, sorrow, and death beat in vain.

God, divine good, does not kill humanity in order to give us eternal Life, for God alone is our life. It is evil that dies; good doesn't die. No matter where you are in the universe, God is the center and circumference of existence.

All forms of error defend two separate antagonistic entities and beings, two powers—namely, Spirit and matter—resulting in a third person (human being) who carries out the delusions of sin, sickness, and death. All forms of error support the false conclusions that there is more than one Life. Material history is not as real and living as spiritual history. Temporary evidence can't uphold mortal error to be as conclusively real as immortal Truth.

The power of Spirit is admitted to be good, an intelligence or Mind called God. To think there is a second power, evil, is to suppose there is something unlike good. If the second power is unlike Mind then it is not intelligence. A third power is believed to be a human being, a

---

[47]   John 19:7

supposed mixture of the first and second antagonistic powers, a mix of intelligence and non-intelligence, of Spirit and matter.

The theories that include many powers are erroneous and don't stand the test of divine Science. Judging them by their fruits, they are rotten. When will you understand your spiritual beingness and realize there is only one God, one Mind or intelligence?

False and self-assertive theories have given sinners the notion that they can create what God cannot—namely, sinful mortals in God's image. This attitude takes God's name without the nature of the image of divine Mind. In Science, it is not true that people have a mind of their own, distinct from God. Everyone reflects, uniquely, the *all* Mind.

It is pantheistic to believe God lives in matter. The error which says that Soul is in body, Mind is in matter, and good is in evil, must stop. Pantheism causes human beings to stumble with lameness, drop with drunkenness, lean on matter, and consume with disease—all because of spiritual blindness, their false perception concerning God and God's children. Spiritual enlightenment confirms that God will not continue to be hidden from humanity.

When will the error of believing that there is life in matter and that sin, sickness, and death are creations of God be exposed? When will it be understood that the inventions of human mind have no intelligence, life, or sensation? When will it be known that the prolific source of all suffering is the insistence that matter/energy has life and intelligence? God created all through Mind, and made all perfect and eternal. It is a belief to think we need to be created again.

We have a difficult time glimpsing God when we get confused or distracted by material energy. So, adjust the out-of-tune thinking and get in tune with Truth. We can then perceive the divine image in some word or deed, which indicates the true idea—the supremacy and reality of good, the nothingness and unreality of evil.

The divine law of loving our neighbor as ourselves unfolds as we realize that there is one Mind. On the flip side, a belief in many ruling minds hinders humanity's advancement toward the one Mind, one God. The assumption that there are numerous minds takes us down dead end roads where selfishness dominates.

Selfishness pulls the weight of human existence toward the side of error, not toward Truth. Denying the oneness of Mind also causes our energy to be put on the wrong side, not of Spirit, good, but of matter, mortality.

When we fully understand our relation to the Divine, we can have no other Mind—no other Love, wisdom, or Truth. In the divine relationship, there is no other sense of Life and no consciousness of the existence of matter or error.

It is only productive to exercise human will-power in subordination to Truth. Human-will has the tendency to misguide our decisions and bring out inferior tendencies. It is the function of spiritual sense to direct man and woman. Mistaken human thoughts injure our body, and even injure others.

Human will-power is liable to all evil. The willfulness of human mind can never heal the sick. Contrastingly, the exercise of spirituality—hope, faith, love—is the prayer of the righteous. The prayer governed by Science instead of human mortal selfhood, heals.

In our scientific relationship to God, we find that whatever blesses one blesses all. Jesus showed with the loaves and the fishes[48] that Spirit, not matter, is the source of supply.

Does God give the parent a child, then give the child sickness to take it away by death? Can there be any birth or death for the spiritual image and likeness of God? Instead of God sending sickness and death, Spirit destroys them, and brings to light spirituality, of which there is no sickness and death. Omnipotent and infinite Mind made all and includes all. This Mind does not make mistakes and subsequently correct them. God does not cause us to sin, to be sick, or to die.

Does God create anew what Life has already created? Nothing is new to God. The Scriptures are definite on this point, declaring that God's work was *finished*,[49] and that it was *good*.[50]

There are evil beliefs, often called evil spirits; however, these evils are not Spirit, for there is no evil in Spirit. As we advance spiritually, evil becomes more apparent and obnoxious. Continuing to advance spiritually, material evil will disappear from our lives, because God

---

[48]   Matt. 14:19; Matt. 15:36; Mark 6:44; Mark 8:6 Luke 9:16; John 6:11

[49]   Gen. 2:2

[50]   Gen. 1:31

is Spirit, reality. This fact proves our position, for every scientific affirmation in Christianity has its proof. Error of statement leads to error in action.

God is not the creator of an evil mind. Indeed, evil is not Mind. We must learn that evil is the awful deception and unreality of existence. Evil is not supreme; good is not helpless; nor are the so-called laws of matter primary and the law of Spirit secondary. Without this lesson, we lose sight of the perfect Source, or the divine Principle of spiritual selfhood.

Body is not first and Soul last, nor is evil mightier than good. The Science of being rejects self-evident impossibilities, such as the alliance of Truth and error in cause or effect. Science separates the weeds and wheat in time of harvest.[51]

There is but one original cause. Therefore there can be no effect from any other cause, and there can be no reality in aught which does not proceed from this great and only cause. Sin, sickness, disease, and death belong not to the Science of being. Human beings ultimately cannot create their own reality—cannot presume the absence of spiritual Truth, Life, or Love.

The spiritual reality is the scientific fact in all things. The spiritual fact, repeated in the action of person and the whole universe, is harmonious and is the ideal of Truth. Spiritual facts are not really reversed. The contraposition, which bears no resemblance to spirituality, is not real. The only evidence of a reversal comes from the ever-supposing error, which offers no proof of God, Spirit, or of the spiritual creation. Human perceptions define all things temporally and have a finite sense of the infinite.

The Scriptures say, "For in him we live and move and have our being."[52] What then is this seeming power, independent of God, which causes disease and cures it? It is mortal thinking being projected outward—a law of human mind, a mistaken power, wrong in every sense, embracing sin, sickness, and death. The ostensible power of mortal thinking is the complete contrast to sacred Mind, to Truth, and to spiritual law. Temporal law has no agreement with the goodness of God's character. Soul cannot decide to make children sick and then

---

[51] Matt. 13:36-39
[52] Acts 17:28

30

leave the children to heal themselves. It is absurd to suppose that matter can both cause and cure disease or that Spirit, God, produces disease and leaves the remedy to matter.

Joyce Meyer wrote in her book *The Battlefield of the Mind*, "The mind is the leader or forerunner of all actions."[53] Statements such as these lead thought to look past the superficial, they are as a "voice of one calling in the desert,"[54] preparing humanity for the real and eternal. Let us come to know the way of divine Science. Let us prepare for the supremacy of Spirit, the kingdom of heaven—the government and law of universal harmony, which cannot be lost or remain forever unseen.

Mind, not matter, is causation. A material body only expresses a temporal and human mind. Human beings possess this body and make it harmonious or discordant according to the images of thought imprinted upon it. You embrace your body in your thought. Be sure to outline on the body thoughts of health, not of sickness. Make the effort to banish all thoughts of disease and sin and of other beliefs connected to mortality. Man and woman, being spiritual, have a perfect indestructible life. It is the mortal thinking which makes the body disordered and diseased in proportion as spiritual unawareness, *fear,* or human-will governs human beings.

Mind, supreme over all its formations and governing them all, is the central sun of its own systems of ideas. God is the life and light of all its own expanding creation; and we are tributary to divine Mind. The measurable human body or mind is not God's child.

The world would collapse without Mind, without the intelligence which holds the "winds"[55] in its grasp. Neither philosophy nor skepticism can hinder the movement of Science, which is revealing the supremacy of Mind. The intuitive sense of Mind-power reinforces the glory of Mind. Nearness, not distance, lends delight to this view.

Quantum mechanics; water on Mars; the structures and reactions of molecules; the patterns and relationships between masses and forces; wavelengths and so on, are of no real importance, when we remember that they all must give place to the spiritual fact by the translation of the

---

53   Meyer, Joyce. *Battlefield of the Mind: Winning the Battle in Your Mind.* New York: Warner, 1995.

54   Isa. 40:3; Matt. 3:3; Mark 1:3; Luke 3:4

55   Rev. 7:1

universe and man and woman back into Spirit. As this transformation occurs, our true selfhood and the universe will be found harmonious and spiritual.

Genome sequences, seismic surveys, radiometric dating, information from satellites and space stations, and the paradigms of speculative theories, all based on the hypothesis of physical law, or life and intelligence resident in matter, will ultimately fade away in the presence of the infinite calculus of Spirit.

Spiritual sense is a conscious, constant capacity to understand God. Spiritual sense shows the supremacy of faith "accompanied by action,"[56] over faith in words. Spiritual ideas are expressed only in "new tongues."[57] These ideas are interpreted by the translation of the spiritual original into the language which human thought can comprehend.

Spiritual sense discerns the Principle and proof of the manifestation of God. Jesus was instrumental in setting forth Principle. His Christ-like proofs showed—by healing the sick, driving out evils, and destroying death ("the last enemy to be destroyed"[58]), his disregard of human mind and its fragmented laws.

Knowing that the attributes of Soul were forever manifested through man and woman, the Teacher gave sight to the blind, hearing to the deaf, feet to the lame, and healed the sick. Christ Jesus brought to light the scientific action of the divine Mind on human minds and bodies. He gave a better understanding of Soul and salvation. Jesus healed sickness and sin by one and the same metaphysical process.

The expression *human mind* is really a grammatical error, because Mind is spiritual, not material. Spirit, Truth, pierces the ambiguous error of materiality as a sunbeam penetrates the cloud. Error, mortality, will always "sow the wind and reap the whirlwind."[59] The human mind is mortal, self-destructive, because it can't obey or disobey the spiritual law of Life, Truth.

What is termed matter, being unintelligent, cannot say, "I suffer, I die, I am sick, or I am well." It is the so-called human mind which voices this and appears to make good its claim. To human sense, sin

---

[56] James 2:17
[57] Mark 16:17
[58] I Cor. 15:26
[59] Hosea 8:7

and suffering are real, but spiritual sense includes no evil or epidemic. Because spiritual sense has no error of sense, it has no sense of error; therefore it is without a destructive element.

Who will say whether Truth or error is greater? Are brain, nerves, and the stomach, intelligent? If they talk to us, tell us their condition and report how they feel—then Spirit and matter, Truth and error, commingle and produce sickness and health, good and evil, life and death.

It is provable that Mind, God, is not mortal. Is it not equally true that mortal mind and its temporal projections do not appear in the spiritual understanding of being? Does matter have sensation? The sensations of the body must either be the sensations of human mind or of matter. Nerves are not mind.

The sensation of sickness and the impulse to sin seem to come by the human mind. When a tear starts, doesn't this so-called mind produce the effect seen in the lacrimal gland? Without human mind, the tear could not appear; and this action shows the nature of all material cause and effect.

Do not fall back on the saying that "the fathers have eaten sour grapes, and the children's teeth are set on edge."[60] Sympathy with error should disappear. Science renders impossible the transfer of mistaken thoughts from one mind to another.

Is it true that nerves have sensation? Does matter have intelligence? Do the material organs cause the eyes to see and the ears to hear? If so, when the body is dematerialized, these faculties must be lost, for their immortality is not in Spirit. The fact is, that only through dematerialization and spiritualization of thought, can these faculties be conceived of as immortal.

Nerves are not the source of pain or pleasure. We suffer or enjoy in our dreams, but this pain or pleasure is not communicated through a nerve. Why, after pulling a bad tooth, can there sometimes be a continued belief of a toothache? What about phantom limb? There is a feeling, but no nerves. If the feeling can return, or be prolonged, why can't the limb reappear?

Why does pain rather than pleasure, usually come to human perception? The memory of pain is more vivid than the memory of

---

[60] Jer. 31:29; Ez. 18:2

pleasure. I have seen an unconscious attempt to scratch the end of a finger which had been amputated. When the nerve is gone, which we say was the occasion of pain, and the pain still remains, it proves sensation to be in the human mind, not in matter. Reverse the process; take away this so-called mind instead of a piece of the flesh, and the nerves have no sensation.

Human beings have a modus of their own, not directed and not sustained by God. They produce a rose through seed or grafts, and bring the rose into contact with the olfactory nerves that they may smell it. In the meantime, they automatically believe that organized matter produced the flower. God alone makes and clothes the lilies of the field,[61] and this is done by means of Mind, not matter.

Because all the methods of Mind are not understood, we say the lips or hands must move in order to convey thought. We think wave/particles are necessary to convey sound, or even that other methods involve so-called miracles. The realities of being, its normal action and the origin of all things, are unseen to human sense and maybe even believed to be unreal, while the imaginary or artificial movements of human belief, which would reverse the spiritual modus and action, are styled the real. Whoever contradicts the human minds supposed reality is called a deceiver, or is said to be deceived. It has been said of human beings, "As he thinks in his heart, so is he."[62] As we spiritually *understand*, so are we in truth.

Human mind conceives of something as gas, liquid, solid, granular, or condensate, and then classifies it quantitatively. Infinite and spiritual facts exist apart from this mortal and material conception and projection. God, good, is self-existent and self-expressed, though indefinable as a whole. Every step toward spirituality is a departure from materiality and is a tendency toward God, Spirit. Material theories partially paralyze this attraction toward infinite and eternal good by a distraction to the measurable, flamboyant, and chaotic.

The physical ear does not really hear. Sound is a mental impression made on human belief. Divine Science reveals sound as communicated through the senses of Soul—through spiritual understanding.

---

[61] Matt. 6:28; Luke 12:27
[62] Prov. 23:7 (Amplified)

Mozart experienced more than he expressed. The exquisiteness of his grandest symphonies was never heard. He was a musician beyond what the world knew. This was even more strikingly true of Beethoven, who was for so long hopelessly deaf. Mental melodies and tones of sweet music supersede conscious sound. Music is the rhythm of head and heart. Human mind is the harp of many strings, conferring either discord or harmony, depending on whether the hand which sweeps over it is human or divine.

Trust your spiritual experiences; even if it is difficult to express them.

To believe in beginnings and endings is to abandon divine Mind as infinite Being. Before human-made learning plunged into the depths of a false perception of things, it is possible that the impressions from Truth were as distinct as sound, and that they came as sound to the primitive prophets. If the instrument of hearing is wholly spiritual, it is normal and indestructible.

Enoch's perception was not confined to the evidence before his physical senses. Therefore, he "walked with God"[63]—he ascended—Enoch was guided into the demonstration of life eternal.

Adam, represented in the Scriptures as formed from dust, is a case in point for the human mind. The physical senses, like Adam, originate in matter and return to dust—are proved non-intelligent. Limited senses go out as they came in, for they are still the error, not the truth of being. When it is learned that the spiritual sense, and not the material, conveys the impressions of Mind, then being will be understood and found to be harmonious.

We lend our self to matter and entertain limited thoughts of God the same as unbelievers do with their false gods. Human beings are inclined to fear and to obey what they consider a material body more than they do a spiritual God. All knowledge based on matter, like the original "tree of knowledge,"[64] multiplies our pains, for mortal illusions would rob God and kill us. In the meantime, temporary knowledge spreads like cancer and gives thanks.

---

[63] Gen. 5:24; Heb. 11:5

[64] Gen. 2:9

How unreliable is mortal sight when a wound on the retina may end the power of light and lens! But the real sight or sense is not lost. Accidents, or getting older, can't interfere with the senses of Soul, and there are no other real senses. Evidence confirms that the body, as matter, has no sensation of its own, and there is no oblivion for Soul and its faculties. Spirit's senses are without pain and they are forever at peace. Nothing can hide from spiritual sense the harmony of all things and the might and permanence of Truth.

If Spirit, Soul, could sin or be lost, then being and immortality would be lost, along with all the faculties of Mind; but being cannot be lost while God exists. Soul and matter stand apart from the very necessity of their opposite natures. Humanity is unacquainted with the reality of existence, because matter and mortality do not reflect the facts of Spirit.

Spiritual vision is not dependent on a physical location or person. Whatever is governed by God is never for an instant deprived of the light and might of intelligence and Life.

We are sometimes led to believe that darkness is as real as light. Science affirms darkness to be only a human sense of the absence of light. Darkness loses the appearance of reality in the presence of light. So sin and sorrow, disease and death, are the supposed absence of Life, God, and vanish before truth and love.

With its divine proof, Science reverses the evidence of limited sense. Every quality and condition of mortality is swallowed up in spirituality. Mortals are the opposite of immortals in origin, in existence, and in their relation to God.

Socrates[65] did not fear the hemlock poison, because he understood the superiority and immortality of good. The faith of his philosophy treated physical timidity with contempt. Having pursued spirituality, Socrates recognized the immortality of man and woman. Although Socrates was worthy of respect, the ignorance and malice of that time would have killed him because of his faith in Soul and his indifference to the body.

Who will say that God's children are alive today, but may be dead tomorrow? What has touched Life, God, to such strange issues? Here

---

[65] Socrates, (469-399BC) Greek philosopher. Charged, tried, and condemned to die in 399BC.

theories cease, and Science unveils the mystery and solves the problem of man and woman. Error strikes the heel of truth, but cannot kill truth. Truth crushes the head[66] of error—destroys error. Spirituality lays open siege to materialism. On which side are we fighting?

The understanding that the Ego, I AM, is Mind, and that there is but one Mind or intelligence, begins at once to destroy the errors of human sense and to supply the truth of spiritual sense. This understanding makes the body harmonious; it makes the nerves, bones, brain, etc., servants, instead of masters. If humanity is governed by the law of divine Mind, the body is obedient to everlasting Life and Truth and Love. The great mistake of human beings is to suppose that person, God's image and likeness, is both matter and Spirit, both good and evil.

If the decision were left to the physical senses, evil would appear to be the master of good and sickness to be the rule of existence. Health is not the exception, death is not the inevitable, and life is not pointless. Paul asked: "How can there be harmony between Christ and the devil?"[67]

When we say things like, "My body is physical; my body is a shell," I say with Paul: Be "away from the body and at home with the Lord."[68] Give up your temporal belief that mind is in brain and have but one Mind, even God; for this Mind forms its own likeness. You will not lose your identity through the understanding which Science gives. The possibility of a lost identity is more absurd than to conclude that individual musical tones are lost in the origin of harmony.

Medical schools may inform us that the healing work of Christian Science—which proves Mind to be scientifically distinct from matter—implies an unnatural mental state. We could also be told that Paul's Christian conversion and experience indicated an abnormal mental and bodily condition, even catalepsy and hysteria. Notwithstanding, if we turn to the Scriptures, what do we read? "If anyone keeps my word, he will never see death."[69] And "Regard no one from a worldly point of view."[70]

---

66 Gen. 3:15
67 II Cor. 6:15 (Phillips NT)
68 II Cor. 5:8
69 John 8:51
70 II Cor. 5:16

That scientific methods are superior to others is seen by their effects. When you have conquered a diseased condition of the body through Mind, that condition never recurs and you advanced in divine Science. For example, when purified mentality gives rest to the body, the next toil will fatigue you less, for you are working out the problem of being in divine metaphysics. The scientific and permanent remedy for fatigue is to learn the power of Mind over the body or over any illusion of physical weariness. Material particles cannot be weary and stressed. Remember, in proportion as you understand the control which Mind has over materialized human mind, you will be able to demonstrate this control.

You say, "This job tires me." But what is this *me*? Is it muscle or mind? Which is fatigued and so speaks? Without mind, could the muscles be tired? Do the muscles talk, or do you talk for them? Matter is non-intelligent. Human mind does the false talking and that which affirms weariness, made that weariness.

You do not say a moving wheel is fatigued; and yet the body is as material as the wheel. Like the wheel, the body would never be weary, except for when the human mind says it is. The consciousness of Truth rejuvenates us more than hours of unconsciousness.

The body assumes to say, "I am ill." The reports of sickness may form a coalition with the reports of sin, and say, "I am revenge, lust, appetite, envy, hate." Sin and sickness are difficult to cure because the human mind is the sinner, refusing self-correction. Human mind insists the body can be sick independently of itself and that the divine Mind has no jurisdiction over the body.

Why pray for the recovery of the sick, if you are without faith in God's willingness and ability to heal? If you do believe in God, why do you substitute drugs for the Almighty's power? Why employ means which lead only into temporary, material ways of obtaining help, instead of turning in time of need to God, divine Love, who is an ever-present, permanent help?

Treat a thought of sickness as you would sin, with sudden refusal. Resist the temptation to believe in matter as intelligent, as having sensation or power.

The Scriptures say, "Those who look to the Lord will win new strength, they will soar as on eagles' wings; they will run and not feel faint, march on and not grow weary."[71] The meaning of that passage is not perverted by applying it literally to moments of fatigue, for the moral and physical are as one in their results. When we wake to the truth of being, all disease, pain, weakness, weariness, sorrow, sin, death, will be unknown, and the mortal dream will forever cease. My method of treating fatigue applies to all bodily ailments, since Mind should be, and is, supreme, absolute, and final.

In mathematics, we do not multiply when we are to subtract, and then say the answer is correct. No more can we say in Science that muscles give strength, or that nerves give pain or pleasure, or that genes and chemicals govern, and then expect that the result will be harmony. Material muscles, nerves, DNA, or bones are nothing without mind, but human mind keeps beating its head "against brick walls,"[72] whereas divine Mind heals.

When divine Mind's action is understood, we will never affirm concerning the body what we do not wish to experience. We will not call the body weak, if we would have it strong. The belief in feebleness must obtain in the human mind before it can be made manifest on the body. As the thinking that we are weak is removed, so are its effects. Science includes no rule of disorder, but governs harmoniously. "The wish," wrote Shakespeare "is ever father to the thought."[73]

We may hear a sweet melody and yet misunderstand the science that governs it. Those who are healed through metaphysical Science may not understand the Principle of the cure. They may even impute their recovery to change of air or diet, not rendering to God the honor due to Spirit alone. Entire immunity from the belief in sin, suffering, and death may not be reached at this level, but we may expect a decrease in these evils; and this scientific beginning is in the right direction.

We hear it said: "I exercise every day and take vitamin C so I won't catch a cold. Yet, I always get a cold, have a runny nose, and cough non-stop." Admitting this is a first step to opening the mind to the futility of constantly paying attention to the material body. As a result of the futility, thought is nudged to look in other more effective directions for cause and cure.

---

[71]   Isa. 40:31 (REB)
[72]   Isa. 1:5 (The Message)
[73]   Shakespeare, William, (1564-1616) *Henry IV*, part 2, act IV, sc. 5, line 91.

Instinct is better than misguided reason, even as nature declares. The violet lifts her blue eye to greet the early spring. The leaves clap their hands as nature's lively worshippers. The snowbird sings and soars amid the wind gusts. Birds do not catch a cold from wet feet; securing a summer residence with ease. Earth's atmosphere is kinder than the atmosphere of human mind—kinder than the milieu crowded with thoughts of flu, colds, and allergies. Sicknesses and contagion are produced solely by human theories.

Human mind procreates its own phenomena, and then credits them to something else—like a kitten glancing into the mirror at itself and thinking it sees another kitten.

A minister once adopted a diet of bread and water to increase his spirituality. Finding his health failing, he gave up his abstinence and advised others never to try dietetics for growth in grace.

The mistake of thinking that either fasting or feasting makes us better morally or physically is one of the fruits of "the tree of the knowledge of good and evil," concerning which God said, "you must not eat from."[74] Human mind forms all conditions of the human body and controls the organs, bones, genes, cells, blood, etc., as directly as the determination or will moves the hand.

I knew a person who when quite a child adopted a whole wheat and vegetarian diet to cure indigestion. For many years, he ate only bread and vegetables, and drank nothing but water. His dyspepsia increasing, he decided that his diet should be more rigid. So, he ate only one meal every twenty-four hours, a meal consisting of only a thin slice of bread. His physician also recommended that he should not moisten his extremely dry throat until three hours after eating. The person passed many weary years in hunger and weakness, almost in starvation. The skill of the doctors was exhausted and they kindly informed him that death was indeed his only alternative, so he finally made up his mind to die. Then divine Science saved him, and perfect health was restored without a reminder of the old complaint.

This person learned that suffering and disease were the self-imposed beliefs of mortals, and not the facts of being. He recognized that God never decreed dis-ease—never ordained a law that fasting should be a means of health. These truths opened the sufferer's eyes, relieved

74   Gen. 2:17

his stomach, and he ate without suffering, "giving God thanks;" but he never enjoyed his food as he had imagined he would when he felt hungry and was not disciplined by self-denial and divine Science. Also, although having compassion for starving people around the world, he had learned something more than food was necessary to solve our human predicament.

Taking less thought about what he ought to eat or drink, consulting the stomach less and God more about the best way to live, he recovered strength and flesh rapidly. For many years he had been kept alive, as was believed, only by the strictest attention to fleshly health, and yet he continued ill all the while. After dropping drugs and his routine of severe dieting, he gave his attention to spiritual health, acted according to the improved mentality, and was well.

Another lesson he learned was, that an afflicted person was nowhere close to being the image and likeness of God—nowhere close to being able to "rule over the fish of the sea and the birds of the air and over every living creature that moves on the ground,"[75] especially if eating a bit of animal flesh could overpower him. He finally concluded that God never made indigestion, while fear, diet, physiology, and physics did, contrary to God's order.

Semi-starvation or anorexia is not acceptable to wisdom and it is equally far from Science in which being is sustained by God, Mind. Food has less power to help or to hurt us after thought has transformed to the spiritual. Without the consent of human mind, food and the stomach can't make you suffer. This new-born understanding brings with it another lesson, that self-indulgence, gluttony, or bulimia, are sensual illusions and can't give you satisfaction. It is a human deception to believe you have to eat if you feel hungry. It is another deception to believe purging food will help you stay skinny. As human deceptions disappear we better understand our spiritual existence and ascend the mountain of a balanced life.

Food affects the body only as fleshly mind has its material methods of working. One method is to believe that proper food supplies nutriment and strength to the human system. The human mind's recipe for health never gets it right, whereas Truth regenerates this fleshly mind and feeds thought with the bread of Life.

---

[75] Gen. 1:28

In seeking a cure for digestive and food related problems, don't consult matter. You can eat what is put in front of you, "without raising questions of conscience."[76] We must destroy the false knowledge that life and intelligence are in matter. We must desire to establish ourselves in what is pure and perfect. Paul said, "Walk and live [habitually] in the [Holy] Spirit [responsive to *and* controlled *and* guided by the Spirit]; then you will certainly not gratify the cravings and desires of the flesh (of human nature without God)."[77] Sooner or later we will learn that restraints on our human abilities are pounded into us by the illusion that we live in body instead of in Soul, that we embody mortality instead of immortality.

Physical particle/waves do not express Spirit. God is infinite omnipresent Spirit. If Spirit is *all* and is everywhere, what and where is this limited so-called substance? Remember, truth is greater than error and we cannot put the greater into the lesser. Soul is Spirit, and Spirit is greater than body. If Spirit were once within the body, Spirit would be bound and therefore could not be infinite Spirit.

The question, "What is Truth," convulses the world. Many are ready to meet this inquiry with the assurance which comes of understanding. However, more people are blinded by their old misinterpretations and try to pass the question off. "If one blind person guides another, both will fall into a pit."[78]

The efforts to answer the question, "What is Truth," by some *ology* are vain. Spiritual reasoning and free thought accompany approaching Science, and cannot be put down. Divine logic and mentality will liberate humanity and strategically remove and displace unscientific means and relative laws.

Alarms, that should startle the trance-like thought out of its erroneous dream, are neglected. Marvels, disasters, and sin will increase as human beings are urged to stop resisting the claims of Truth. The awful daring of sin destroys sin and foreshadows the triumph of truth—the last trump sounded. God will turn it over again and again, until "He comes whose right it is."[79] Longevity is increasing and the

---

[76] I Cor. 10:25, 27
[77] Gal. 5:16 (Amplified)
[78] Matt. 15:14 (NRSV)
[79] Ezk. 21:27 (NASB)

power of sin diminishing, for the world feels the renewing effect of truth through every pore.

As the primitive footprints of the past disappear from the dissolving paths of the present, we shall better understand the Science which governs these changes and stand on firmer ground. Every sensuous pleasure or pain is self-destroyed through suffering. There can be painless progress, attended by life and peace instead of disorder and death.

Throughout history, there are many religions but not enough spirituality. Religionists are ready to call on an anthropomorphic God. They were, and are, ready to delegate power to, and lavish with majesty, the human-like God. However, this is not the manner of truth's appearing. Centuries ago, and today, the cross is truth's central sign. The Roman era whip was more material than the modern whip of today, but they are both as equally cutting. Cold contempt, stubborn resistance, opposition from church, state laws, and the press, still try to stop truth's full-orbed appearing.

A higher and more practical Christianity, demonstrating justice and meeting the needs of human beings in sickness and in health, stands at the door of this age, knocking for admission. Will you open or close the door upon this angel visitor? Will you welcome the angel who comes quietly, unpretentiously?

Truth encourages the elements of freedom. The Soul-inspired headline reads, "Mental Manipulation Eliminated." The power of God focuses the attention on spiritual deliverance. No power can withstand divine Love. What or who is it

> Self-help is a good start, but the human self can't deliver. Ultimately, the human mind is delivered from itself by divine Mind.

that makes the rules of depression and exploitation? What is it that draws us away from Spirit? How do we become saddled by wants and whims? What is it that holds human beings in the clutches of sin, sickness, and death? Truth makes us free.

At first, Truth leads the few and faithful. As time marches on, these few and faithful thoughts of Truth move forward with the motto of freedom. The powers of this world will react and the old-guard will try to stop truth and make it submit to their human standards and systems. Science, not distracted by threats or assaults, continues to progress. There is always some chaos; however a mobilization to truth's standard is inevitable.

Improvement comes as mindsets improve. World history illustrates the might of Mind and shows human power to be proportionate to its embodiment of right thinking or spiritual clarity. Words and actions, breathing the omnipotence of divine justice and wisdom, are what powerfully break the grip of discrimination, human agendas, and diminishing returns. Mental fogginess doesn't go down in blood, nor does the breath of freedom come from the weapons of humans. Love is the liberator.

Legally to abolish terrorism in the world is difficult, but the elimination of mental terrors is a more difficult task. The domineering tendencies inherent in the human mind, and always germinating in new forms of tyranny, must be rooted out through the action of the divine Mind.

Men and women of all environments and cultures are still under the control of terrorists and bullies, ignorant how to obtain their freedom. However, the rights of humanity are being vindicated as people fight for equal rights and remove dictators from office. Moreover, this is prophetic of further steps coming toward the banishment of world-wide oppression, found on higher planes of existence and under more subtle and depraving forms.

The voice of God in behalf of the people is reverberating around the world as the spokesperson of this new crusade sounds the keynote of universal mental freedom. A fuller acknowledgement of the rights of man and woman as useful spiritual beings demands that the terrors of sin, sickness, and death be exterminated from the human mind. Not through human warfare, not with borders and anger, but through spiritual Science is freedom gained.

God has built a higher platform of human rights on divine claims. These claims are not made through human regulations or creeds, but in demonstration of "Peace upon earth among men of goodwill!"[80] Human policies, scholastic theology, human health care systems put our faith and spiritual understanding in hand cuffs.

---

80   Luke 2:14 (Phillips NT)

Divine Science rescues us, and our birthright of sole allegiance to our Maker asserts itself.

The children of Israel can be saved from the bureaucracies and educational systems of today's Pharaohs. The disabled, the deaf, the dumb, the visually impaired, the sick, the sensualist, the sinner, can be saved from the terrors of their own beliefs. When I saw the sick, wearing out years of servitude to an unreal master in the belief that the body governed them, rather than Mind, I wanted to help. I saw before me the awful conflict, the Red Sea and the wilderness; however, I pressed on through faith in God, trusting Truth, the strong deliverer, to guide thought into the land of divine Science. In this land, or state of consciousness, limitations are overcome and the rights of man and woman are fully known and acknowledged.

Oppressive laws are disputed and human beings are taught their right to freedom. From this same standpoint, it becomes obvious that erroneous human beliefs and the claims of the self-sabotaging physical senses must be disputed and replaced. The law of the divine Mind must end human repression, or human beings will continue to be unaware of their inalienable rights. People will be prone to hopeless obsessions or to become enablers because some public teachers permit an unawareness of divine power—an unawareness true responsibility and freedom.

Discerning the rights of people, we can't fail to foresee the doom of all oppression. Uselessness and backwardness are not legitimate states. God made us free. Paul said, "I was born a citizen."[81] Humanity should be free to help themselves and society. "Where the Spirit of the Lord is, there is freedom."[82] Love and Truth make free, whereas evil and error lead into captivity.

Divine Science raises the standard of freedom and says: "Follow me! Escape from the control of sickness, sin, and death!" Jesus designated the way. Citizens of the world, accept the "glorious freedom of the children of God,"[83] and be free! This is your divine right. The self-deluded idolatrous views, not divine law, has captivated you, made

---

[81]   Acts 22:28

[82]   II Cor. 3:17

[83]   Rom. 8:21

you arthritic, made you a procrastinator, weakened your body, and ruined your reputation.

God did not institute physical laws to control us. We do not have to get sick if we disobey a human-made health law. Jesus healed in direct opposition to, and in defiance of, all material laws and conditions. Jesus would not have disregarded any of God's governing laws.

Genetics is a prolific subject for human belief to attach theories to; but if we learn that nothing is real but the right, we shall have no dangerous inheritances and fleshly ills will disappear. It would be impossible to transmit disease or certain human traits if this great fact of being was learned—namely, that nothing inharmonious can enter being, for Life *is* God.

To be dependent on that which is constantly changing is not legitimate. False dependencies will cease as we recognize our God-given dominion over the temporal senses and enter into our heritage of freedom. Human beings will someday assert their freedom in the name of Almighty God. Dropping our present beliefs, we will recognize harmony as the spiritual reality, and disorder as the temporal unreality, and then control our own bodies through the understanding of divine Science.

Jesus said, "Do not worry about your life."[84] If we follow the direction of Jesus, we can depend less and less on bodily conditions, structure, or economy. We can be masters of the body, dictate its features, and form and control it with Truth.

There is no power apart from Mind. Omnipotence has all-power, and to acknowledge any other power is to dishonor God. The humble Nazarene overthrew the assumption that sin, sickness, and death have power. He proved them powerless. It should have humbled the arrogance of the priests when they saw the demonstration of spirituality excel the influence of their dead faith and ceremonies.

If Mind is not supreme over sin, sickness, and death, they are immortal. Particle/waves are the basis and support of sin and disease. Matter/energy has yet to prove it can destroy sin and disease.

---

[84] Matt. 6:25; Luke 12:22

We should hesitate to say that Yahweh sins or suffers. If sin and suffering are realities of being, how did they first come about? God made all that was made, and Mind signifies God—infinity, not finity. The belief which unites opposites such as sickness and health is not far removed from infidelity. To believe that holiness comes into contact with that which is unholy—calling both the offspring of spirit, and at the same time admitting that Spirit is God—virtually declares God is good in one instance and evil in another.

> False: God punishes our impatience by making us sick.
> True: God removes impatience by giving us more patience.

By universal consent, the mortal mindset has constituted itself a law to obligate human beings to sickness, sin, and death. This programmed mindset and the individual who upholds it is mistaken in theory and in practice. The so-called law of human mind, conjectural and speculative, is made void by the law of spiritual Mind. Be sure to trample false law under foot.

If God causes people to be sick, sickness must be good, and therefore health must be evil, for all that He makes is good and will stand forever. Or, if violating God's law produces sickness, it is right to be sick; and we cannot if we would, and should not if we could, annul the decrees of wisdom. However, it is the transgression of a belief of human mind, not of a law of matter nor of divine Mind, which causes the belief of sickness. The remedy is Truth, not mortality—the truth that disease is illusion, *unreal.*

If sickness is real, it belongs to spirituality; if true, it is a part of Truth. Would you attempt with drugs, or without, to destroy a quality or condition of Truth? On the flipside, if sickness and sin are unfiltered and unprocessed images, divine Science can filter and process the images and bring us back into health, holiness, and spirituality. This process or clarification of information is accomplished through Spirit, Christ, or the advanced appearing of Truth which is benefiting people and healing the sick. This is the salvation which comes through God, the divine Principle, Love, as demonstrated by Jesus.

It would be contrary to our highest ideas of God to suppose She makes unwise decisions, or is capable of arranging law and causation so as to bring about certain evil results, punishing helpless victims for doing what they could not avoid doing. Good is not, cannot be, the author of experimental sins. God, good, can no more produce sickness than goodness and health can decide to be evil and diseased.

Does wisdom make gross mistakes which must afterward be corrected by man or woman? Does a law of God produce sickness, and can we put that law under our feet by healing sickness? According to Holy Writ, the sick are never really healed by drugs, hygiene, or any material method. These merely evade the question and are soothing syrups to put children to sleep, satisfy human belief, and avoid fear.

We think that we are healed when a disease disappears, though it is liable to reappear. We are never thoroughly healed until the liability to be ill is removed. The human mortal mind is the remote, predisposing, and the stimulating cause of all suffering. Therefore, the cause of disease must be obliterated through Truth in divine Science, or the physical senses will get the victory.

Unless an ill is rightly met and fairly overcome by Truth, the ill is never conquered. If God does not destroy sin, sickness, and death, they are not destroyed in the mind of human beings and seem to be immortal. We do not need to attempt to do what God cannot do. If God does not heal the sick, they are not healed, for no lesser power equals the infinite All-power; however, God, Truth, Life, Love, does heal the sick through the prayer of the righteous.

If God makes sin, if good produces evil, if truth results in error, then Science and Christianity are helpless; but there are no antagonistic powers nor laws (spiritual or material), creating and governing us through perpetual warfare. God is not the author of fleshly disorders. Therefore, we accept the conclusion that disorders have only a fabulous existence and are human beliefs which divine Truth and Love destroy.

To hold yourself superior to backwardness, because God made you superior to it and governs us, is true wisdom. To fear loss is to misunderstand the power of Love and the divine Science of being in our relation to God—to doubt and distrust Soul's omnipotent care. To hold yourself superior to sickness and death is equally wise, and is in accordance with divine Science. To fear them is impossible, when you fully understand God and know that disease and dying are no part of Life's existence.

Under the auspices of our Maker, we can have no other Mind. Secure on the Evangelist's statement that "all things were made; without him nothing was made that has been made,"[85] we can triumph over sin, sickness, and death.

Many theories relative to God and creation do not make a lovable God or harmonious children. The beliefs we commonly entertain about happiness and life actually lack evidence of permanent joy and life. The unspoiled claims of harmonious and eternal being are discovered only in divine Science.

Scripture informs us that "with God all things are possible"[86]—all good is possible to Spirit. Prevalent theories practically deny this and make healing possible only through matter, however, these theories are not true, because all good is possible to God. Christianity is not false, but religions which contradict its Principle are false.

Spirituality is again demonstrating the power of divine Principle as it did over twenty centuries ago, by healing the sick and triumphing over death. Jesus never taught that drugs, food, air, and exercise could make people healthy. Jesus also didn't teach or practice that drugs, food, air, and exercise could destroy human life. He assigned harmony to Mind, not to matter/energy. He was very clear on God's ruling which condemned sin, bad health, and dying.

It is only when the temporary pleasures and pains pass away in our lives that we find unquestionable signs of the burial of error and the resurrection to spiritual life. In the sacred sanctuary of Truth are sincere voices. Are we listening to the spiritual intuitions and following?

There is neither place nor opportunity in Science for error of any sort. Every day makes its demands upon us for better proofs rather than verbal claims of Christian power. These proofs consist solely in the destruction of sin, sickness, and death by the power of Spirit, as

---

[85]   John 1:3
[86]   Matt. 19:26

Jesus destroyed them. This is an element of progress and progress is the law of God whose law demands of us only what we can certainly fulfill.

Surrounded by imperfection, perfection is seen and acknowledged only by degrees. People must slowly work toward perfection. How long it must be before we arrive at the demonstration of scientific being, no person knows—not even "the son, but only the Father."[87] The false claim of error continues its delusions until the goal of goodness is steadfastly earned and won.

Already the shadow of God's right hand rests on the hour. For those of you who "know how to interpret the appearance of the sky,"[88] the physical sign—how much better is it to discern the mental sign? Mental interpretation destroys spiritual unawareness and ill-health by overcoming the thoughts which produce them and by understanding the spiritual idea which corrects and replaces them. Jesus' mission was to reveal the truth of spiritual reality to all humankind, even to the hearts which rejected him.

When numbers have been divided according to a fixed rule, the answer is unquestionable. The scientific tests I have made concerning the effects of truth upon the sick are just as unquestionable. The counter fact relative to any disease is required to cure it. Truth spoken and realized is designed to disprove and destroy error. Why shouldn't truth be efficient in sickness, which is solely the result of disharmony?

Spiritual involvement heals, while material attachment interferes with truth, even as ritualism and creed stifle spirituality. If we trust matter, we distrust Spirit.

Song, sermon, and Science—crumbs of comfort—are capable of inspiring us with wisdom, Truth, and Love. Spiritual comfort blesses the human family, feeds the inner being, and gives living water to the thirsty.

It is most beneficial to become more familiar with good than with evil, and guard against false beliefs as diligently as we bolt our doors against the approach of thieves and murderers. We should love our enemies and help them on the basis of the Golden Rule, "Do to others

---

[87]   Mark 13:32
[88]   Matt. 16:3; Luke 12:56

what you would have them do to you."[89] Avoid throwing "your pearls to pigs,"[90] because then everyone loses out and is deprived.

If humanity would properly guard human mind, the posterity of evils which aggravate it would be cleared out. We must begin with the human mind and empty out its negativity and self-delusion, or negativity and self-delusion will never cease. Human systems and the collection of human-made policies disappoint the weary searcher looking for a divine theology. Human thought is adequately and correctly educated only by spiritual theology.

Sin and disease are thought before they are manifest. You must control evil thoughts in the first instance or they will control you in the second. Jesus declared that to look with desire on forbidden objects was to break a moral precept. He laid great stress on the action of the human mind, unseen to the senses.

Evil thoughts and aims reach no farther and do no more harm than one's thinking permits. Evil thoughts, lusts, and malicious purposes cannot roam around like wandering viruses from one human mind to another finding an unsuspecting host, if virtue and truth build a strong defense. It is important to be aware of the mental environment so as not to be a naive receptor of evil thoughts. You would rather choose a doctor who has the flu to treat you, than be treated mentally by one who does not obey the requirements of divine Science.

Character development should be strongly fortified with virtue. It is not so much academic education, as an ethical and spiritual learning which improves the character of the audience. The pure and uplifting thoughts of teachers, instructors, and speakers, constantly imparted to pupils, reach higher than the heavens of astronomy. Corrupt and dubious minds, though gifted with scholarly attainment, will degrade the characters it should inform and elevate. Strive to see the whole picture when selecting teachers and speakers. It is imperative to consider the instructor's morality along with their credentials and skill level.

Physicians, whom the sick employ in their helplessness, should be models of integrity. They should be wise spiritual guides to health and hope. To the frightened patient on the brink of death, physicians can

---

89   Matt. 7:12
90   Matt. 7:6

be prepared to teach them an understanding of the Truth that is Life. When the soul is willing and the flesh is weak, the patient may be willing to learn of the ever-perpetuating Life and their feet may be planted on the rock of Christ, the true idea of spiritual power.

Clergy, chaplains, and spiritual leaders, observing the world, should advance the standard of Truth. They can inspire their hearers spiritually so that their listeners will love to grapple with a new, right idea and broaden their views. Love of spirituality, rather than love of popularity, should stimulate work and progress. Truth should emanate from the pulpit, but never be strangled there. A special privilege is commissioned in the ministry. How will it be used? The privilege of the ministry should be used sacredly in the interests of humanity, not of sect.

Aren't prestige and profit, rather than the dignity of God's laws, what many leaders pursue? People with inferior motives indirectly lead the furious attacks on people who are purely motivated and who are healing through divine Mind.

A parent is the strongest educator either for or against crime. Parental thoughts form the embryo of another human mind and unconsciously shape it, either after a model that disgusts the parent, or through divine influence "after the pattern for them, which was shown to you on the mountain."[91] Spiritual Science helps us learn of the one Mind and of the availability of good as the remedy for every problem.

Teaching children at the earliest possible time the truths of health and holiness is extremely beneficial. Children are more tractable than adults, and learn more readily to love the simple verities that will make them happy and good. Children can learn that obedience to parents and guardians promotes self-control. Disobedience blights.

Jesus loved little children because of their freedom from wrong and their receptiveness to right. While adults hesitate between two opinions or argue with false beliefs, youth makes easy and rapid strides toward Truth.

A little girl, who had occasionally listened to my explanations, badly wounded her finger. She seemed not to notice it. On being questioned about it she answered ingenuously, "There is no sensation in matter."

---

[91] Ex. 25:40 (NASB)

Running off with happy eyes, she presently added, "Mamma, my finger is not a bit sore."

It might have been months or years before the child's parents would have laid aside their drugs or reached the mental height their little daughter so naturally attained. The more stubborn beliefs and theories of parents often choke the good seed in the minds of themselves and their offspring. Superstition, like "the birds of the air,"[92] snatches away the good seed before it has sprouted.

Teaching children divine Science among their first lessons is useful. This includes monitoring and reducing discussions, theories, or thoughts about sickness. To prevent the experience of error and its sufferings, keep out of the minds of your children either sinful or diseased thoughts. Diseased thoughts are excluded on the same principle as the exclusion of sinful thoughts. This makes divine Science available early on in life.

Some invalids are unwilling to know the spiritual facts or to hear about the deception of temporal things and their supposed laws. They devote themselves a little longer to their material gods and cling to believing there is life and intelligence in mortality. They expect this error to do more for them than they are willing to admit the only living and true God can do. Impatient at your explanation, unwilling to investigate Science, they embrace false thinking and suffer the delusive consequences. Mind-Science however, could purge them of their problems.

Intent and action are not properly valued before they are understood. It is well to wait until those whom you would benefit are ready for the blessing. Science is working changes in personal character as well as in the temporal universe.

To obey the Scriptural command, "Come out from their midst and be separate,"[93] is to invite society's disapproval; but this disapproval, more than approval, enables one to be spiritual. Pope John Paul II said, "We cannot live for the future without intuiting that the meaning of life is greater than temporality and is above it. If the societies and the men of our continent have lost interest in such a meaning, they must

---

[92]   Matt. 13:4; Mark 4:4; Luke 8:5
[93]   II Cor. 6:17 (NASB)

rediscover it."[94] The Biblical Paul realized, "If God is for us, who can be against us?"[95]

To fall away from Truth in times of persecution, shows that we never understood Truth. The voice of wisdom calls a warning from the wedding banquet, "I don't know you."[96] Unimproved opportunities will rebuke us when we attempt to claim the benefits of an experience we have not made our own, try to reap the harvest we have not sown, and wish to enter unlawfully into the labors of others. Truth is not looked for until we suffer severely from error and seek a spiritual remedy for human troubles.

Leaving all for Christ includes forsaking popularity and gaining true Christianity. Any attempt to engage society's friendship in order to gain dominion over humankind comes from worldly weakness.

Society is a foolish juror, listening only to one side of the case. Justice often comes too late to secure a verdict. People with mental work before them have no time for gossip about false law or testimony. To reconstruct timid justice and place the fact above the falsehood, is the work of time.

For Christianity, the cross is the central emblem of history. It is the guiding star in the demonstration of Christian healing—the demonstration by which sin and sickness are destroyed. The sects, who endured the abuse of their predecessors, in turn, may badly treat those who are in advance of creeds.

Material wealth, fame, and social organizations have no authority or influence in the presence of God. We attain clearer views of Principle as we break up cliques, level monetary wealth with honesty, and let worth be judged according to wisdom. We also get better views of humanity as we remove our self from biased personal perceptions.

Wicked human beings are not the rulers of upright neighbors. Let it be understood that success in error is defeat in Truth. The password of divine Science is Scriptural: "Let the wicked abandon their ways and the evil their thoughts."[97]

---

[94]   Excerpt from *Day by Day with Pope John Paul II,* edited by Angelo Pisani, Copyright © 1980 by Piero Gribaudi.
[95]   Rom. 8:31
[96]   Matt. 25:12
[97]   Isa. 55:7 (REB)

To discover our progress, we must learn to what we are attached. Who do we acknowledge and obey as power? If divine Love is becoming nearer, dearer, and more real to us, matter is then submitting to Spirit. The goals we pursue and the spirit we manifest reveal our standpoint and show what we are winning.

Human mind is the acknowledged seat of human motives; it designs limited concepts and produces all bodily malfunctions. Action proceeding from erring human mind is inappropriate and ends in sin, sickness, and death. Appropriate action proceeds from the divine Mind. Those two opposite thought sources never mingle in cause or effect. Imperfect human mind projects outward its own resemblances of which the wise man said, "Everything is meaningless."[98] The perfect Mind expresses perfection, for God is immortal Mind.

Nature voices spiritual law and divine Love, but the human mortal mindset misinterprets nature. Arctic regions, sunny tropics, coral reefs, the Mid-Atlantic Ridge, flowering deserts, and galaxies—all point to Mind, the spiritual intelligence they reflect. The floral apostles are hieroglyphs of Deity. Quantum mechanics, gravity, and the cosmos teach grand lessons. The stars make night beautiful, and the leaf turns naturally toward the light.

In the order of Science, in which the Principle is above what it expresses, all is one grand agreement. Change this statement, suppose Mind to be governed by matter or assume that Soul is in the body and you will lose the keynote of being, and there is continual disagreement. Mind is perpetual motion. Its symbol is the sphere. The rotations and revolutions of the universe of Mind go on eternally.

Humanity moves toward good or evil as time passes. If mortals are not progressive, past failures will be repeated until all wrong work is erased or corrected. If there is any satisfaction in wrongdoing, we must learn to loathe it. If we are now content with spiritual idleness, we must become dissatisfied with it. Remember that humankind must sooner or later, either by suffering or by Science, be convinced of the error that is to be overcome.

The effort to unlearn false perceptions includes forfeiting those views completely. Then error will be submissive to Truth. The divine method of becoming responsible for every thought and action, involves

---

[98]   Eccl. 1:2

unwinding our snarls and learning from experience how to divide between false views and Soul.

"The Lord disciplines those he loves."[99] A person who refuses obedience to God is chastened by Love. People who know and obey God's will, or the demands of divine Science, will run up against the hostility of envy.

Sensual treasures are stored "where moth and rust destroy."[100] Mortality is their doom. Sin breaks in and steals them away, carrying off their superficial joys. The sensualist's feelings are as imaginary, capricious, and unreal as their pleasures. Deceit, jealousy, hypocrisy, selfish ambition, hate, revenge, and so forth, steal away the treasures of Truth. Stripped of its coverings, what a mocking spectacle is sin!

The Bible teaches that Spirit renews and transforms the body. Take away the spiritual meaning of Scripture, and that collection of works can no more help human beings than moonbeams can melt a river of ice. The error of all generations is preaching without practice.

The substance of all commitment is the reflection and demonstration of divine Love—is finding progressive answers to problems and destroying sin and sickness. The Teacher said, "If you really love me, you will keep the commandments I have given you."[101]

The goal, a point beyond faith, is to find the footsteps of Truth, the way to health and spirituality. It is necessary to make a sincere effort to reach the Horeb height where God is revealed. The cornerstone of all spiritual building is purity. Spirit's baptism washes the body of all fleshly impurities and shows that the pure in heart see God. We approach spiritual Life and its demonstration through purity.

It is "easier for a camel to go through the eye of a needle,"[102] than for materialist convictions to enter the kingdom of heaven, eternal harmony. Through repentance, spiritual baptism, and reformation, humanity advances past beliefs and false individuality. It is only a question of time when "they will all know me [God], from the least of them to the greatest."[103] Denying the claims of matter/energy is taking

---

[99]   Heb. 12:6
[100] Matt. 6:19, 20; Luke 12:33
[101] John 14:15 (Phillips NT)
[102] Matt. 19:24; Mark 10:25; Luke 18:25
[103] Jer, 31:34; Heb. 8:11 (Brackets added by Mary Baker Eddy)

an important step toward the joys of Spirit, toward human freedom and the final triumph over the body.

There is but one way to heaven, harmony, and Truth in divine Science shows us this way. It is to know no other reality—to have no other consciousness of life—than good, God and Spirit's reflection. Spiritual harmony, happiness, or Christ-likeness includes ascendancy over physical pain and pleasure.

Self-worship is denser than a solid body. In patient obedience to a patient God, let us labor to dissolve with the universal solvent of Love the congealed mass of error. Let us work to bankrupt selfish-will, self-justification, and self-worship, which are errors that compete against spirituality and are the investors in sin and death.

The divine Science of man and woman is seamless. The seamless garment of Life is Truth. According to the Bible, the facts of being are commonly misconstrued, for it is written: "They divided my garments among them and cast lots for my clothing."[104] However, mere speculation or superstition cannot divide the divine garment, whereas spiritual inspiration can restore every fiber of the Christly garment of righteousness.

The sign-posts of divine Science show the way the Teacher walked. We are required to offer the same proof and not just talk about the walk. We may be able to hide from the world our neglect of putting into practice our spiritual power; however, negligence and hypocrisy have no part in the success of Science and in our demonstration of spiritual good.

The divine Love, which made harmless the poisonous viper, which delivered men from the fiery furnace, boiling oil, and from the jaws of the lion, can not only heal the sick in every era, but also triumph over sin and death. Love honored the demonstrations of Jesus with unsurpassed power and compassion. But the same, "attitude . . . as that of Christ Jesus"[105] must always accompany the letter of Science in order to confirm and repeat the ancient demonstrations of prophets and students of Truth. That those wonders are not more commonly repeated today stems not so much from lack of desire as from lack of spiritual growth.

---

[104] Ps. 22:18; John 19:24
[105] Phil. 2:5

Computer software can't inform the programmer. The stomach, heart, colon, and lymph nodes don't inform us that they are nauseous, diseased, cancerous, or invaded by malignant tumors. If this information is conveyed, human mind conveys it. Negative information certainly doesn't come from immortal Mind and it can't come from inanimate matter/energy. God's "eyes are too pure to look on evil,"[106] and physicality has neither intelligence nor sensation.

Truth has no consciousness of error. Love has no sense of hatred. Life has no partnership with death. Truth, Life, and Love are a law of annihilation to everything unlike themselves, because they declare nothing except God.

Sickness, sin, and death are not the merchandise of Life. Sickness, sin, and death are simulations, virtual realities, which Truth destroys with immortal reality. Inasmuch as God is good and the source of all being, Love does not produce moral or physical deformity. Therefore such deformity is not real, but is illusion—is the mirage of error. Divine Science reveals these grand facts and because of these facts Jesus demonstrated Life, never fearing or obeying error in any form. Perfection does not animate imperfection.

If we were to derive all our conceptions of people from what is seen between the cradle and the grave, happiness and goodness would have no home for us. Bacterium would rob us of the flesh we think is our substance. However, Paul writes: "The law of the Spirit of life set me free from the law of sin and death."[107]

To undergo birth, maturity, and decay is like the beasts and vegetables—answerable to laws of deterioration. If man and woman were dust in the earliest stage of existence, we might admit the hypothesis that people eventually return to that primitive condition; but man and woman is not more or less than God's child.

If man and woman do come from dust, or if they flicker out in death, there must be an instant when God is without the entire manifestation. There cannot be an instant when infinite Mind isn't fully reflected.

In Science, person is not young or old; we have no birth or death; we are not a beast, a vegetable, or an evolving mind; we do not advance

---

[106]   Hab. 1:13
[107]   Rom. 8:2

from mortality to Mind, from the materialist to the spiritual, we do not rise from evil to good, or shift from good to evil. Confessing to a state of mortality throws us headlong into darkness and dogma. Too much is written and produced on that which advocates the picture that it is normal to deteriorate and become helpless. It is better to assign to humanity the everlasting grandeur and immortality of improvement, spiritual power, and prestige.

The error of thinking that we are growing old, and the benefits of destroying that illusion, has noticeable results. Most of us have met someone considered old, but very much young in mind/body/spirit. These people have been interviewed and questioned. Are they lucky? Is it their genes? Is it the food they eat? Maybe or maybe not, however, they usually always attribute their longevity to a positive and loving attitude.

The error of thinking that we are growing old, and the benefits of destroying that illusion, is illustrated in a story published in the London medical magazine *The Lancet*.

Deserted by her lover in her early years, a woman living in England became insane and lost all account of time. Believing that she was still living in the same hour when her lover left her, she did not notice passing years. She stood daily before the window watching for her lover's return. In this mental attitude she remained young. Having no consciousness of time, she literally grew no older. Some American travelers saw her when she was seventy-four and assumed she was a young woman. She had no care-lined face, no wrinkles, no gray hair, but a youthful face. Asked to guess her age, those unacquainted with her history guessed that she was younger than twenty.

Years had not made the English woman old because she had taken no cognizance of passing time. She did not think of herself as growing old. The conviction that she was young was an influence manifest on her body. She could not age while believing herself young, for the mental state governed the physical. Impossibilities never occur. Instances like the English woman's case prove it possible to be young at seventy-four. The significance of that illustration makes it plain that decrepitude is not according to law, nor is it a necessity of nature, but an illusion. The examples of perpetual youth furnish a useful hint to the ingenious mind that might work with more certainty than when Bill Gates[108] tapped into instantaneous and seamless communication and commerce around the globe by means of computers, unrestricted by the obstacles of time/space.

The infinite never began and it will never end. Mind and its formations can never be annihilated. God's child is not on a roller coaster, reeling between evil and good, joy and sorrow, sickness and health, life and death. Life and its faculties are not measured by calendars. The perfect and spiritual are the eternal likeness of their Maker. God's idea by no means has a material origin and has to try desperately to reach Spirit, moving from neophyte to the accomplished. Anything with a material origin is going to stay material; however, our origin, or source, is Spirit.

Measuring life by solar years steals from our prime and gives ugliness to age. The radiant sun of virtue and truth coexists with being. Manhood and womanhood is its eternal noon, undimmed by a declining sun. As the physical and material, the transient sense of beauty fades, the radiance of Spirit illumines spiritual sense with bright and imperishable glories.

Don't keep records of aging. Chronological data is no part of the vast forever. Albums that record births and deaths are so many conspiracies against manhood and womanhood. Measuring and limiting all that is good and beautiful is an age-old habit. If not for that routine, we would enjoy our advanced years and still be vigorous, light-hearted, and full of promise. Governed by spiritual Mind, we are always graceful and noble. Each succeeding year unfolds wisdom, beauty, and holiness.

Life is eternal. We should find this out, and begin the demonstration thereof. Life and goodness are spiritual. Let us then shape our views of existence into loveliness, renewal, and consistency, rather than into decrepitude and loss.

Acute and chronic beliefs reproduce their own types. Acute beliefs of physical life come later on, and are not as disastrous as the chronic beliefs.

---

[108] William Henry Gates III, philanthropist, author, and former CEO and current chairman of Microsoft, (1955-)

I have seen adults regain two of the elements they had lost, sight and teeth. A woman of eighty-five, whom I knew, had a return of sight. Another woman at ninety had new teeth, incisors, cuspids, bicuspids, and one molar. One man at sixty had retained his full set of upper and lower teeth without a decaying cavity.

Beauty, as well as truth, is eternal; but the beauty of material things passes away—fades and vanishes as mortal beliefs. Tradition, education, and fashion form the illusive standards of human beings. Spirituality, exempt from decline or decay, has a glory of its own—the radiance of Soul. People are models of spiritual sense. Our spirituality is designed by perfect Mind and reflects those higher conceptions of loveliness which transcend all false conceptions.

Good looks and refinement are independent of matter. Being possesses its qualities before they are perceived humanly. Beauty is a thing of life. It dwells forever in the eternal Mind and reflects the living God in expression, form, outline, and color. It is Love which paints the petal with countless hues, glances in the warm sunbeam, arches the cloud with the bow of beauty, blazons the night with starry gems, and covers earth with loveliness.

Cosmetic surgery, botox, and body decoration are inadequate substitutes for the attractiveness of spirituality, stunningly and eternally outperforming the aging process.

The recipe for beauty is to have less illusion and more Soul. Retreat from the belief of pain or pleasure in body and advance into the unchanging calm and glorious freedom of spiritual harmony.

Love never loses sight of loveliness. Its halo rests on its object. Isn't it amazing that a friend is always beautiful? Men and women of seasoned years and increased wisdom ought to advance in spirituality and health, instead of lapsing into gloom and doom. Spiritual Mind renews the body with nice features. God supplies the body with beautiful images of thought; which destroy the complaints of mortal sense bent on bringing us to the grave.

Sculptors turn from the marble to their model in order to perfect their conception. We are all sculptors, working at various forms, molding and chiseling thought. What is the model before human mind? Is it imperfection, joy, depression, sin, suffering? Have you accepted the human model? Are you reproducing it? Then you are haunted in your work by vicious sculptors and hideous forms. Don't you hear from all humankind of the imperfect model? The world is continually holding it before your observation. The result is that you are liable to follow those ruinous prototypes, limit your lifework, and adopt into your experience the angular outline and deformity of mortal models.

To remedy this, we must first turn our attention in the right direction and then walk that way. We must form perfect models in thought and look at them continually or we shall never carve them out in grand and noble lives. Allow unselfishness, goodness, mercy, justice, health, holiness, and love to control your mind and body. As the kingdom of heaven is found within, then sin, disease, and death will diminish until they finally disappear.

Let us acknowledge Science. Stop accepting theories based on temporal sense-testimony. Give up imperfect models and illusive icons. Let us have one God, one Mind, and that one perfect, producing Spirit's own models of excellence.

Allow the "male and female"[109] of God's creating to appear. Let us feel the divine energy of Spirit, bringing us into newness of life and recognizing no human or material power as able to destroy. Let us rejoice that we are open to the divine "governing authorities."[110] Such is the true Science of being. Any other theory of Life, or God, is delusive and mythological.

Mind is not the author of delusive soulless substance. Either there is no omnipotence, or omnipotence is the only power. God is infinite substance, and infinity never began, will never end, and includes nothing unlike God. From what source then is soulless matter?

Life is, like Christ, "the same yesterday and today and forever."[111] Organization and time have nothing to do with Life. You say, "I dreamed last night." What a mistake! The "I" is Spirit. God never sleeps and never dreams, so God's likeness is conscious and doesn't dream. Mortals are the Adam dreamers.

Sleep and apathy are dimensions of the dream that life, substance, and intelligence are temporal, measurable. Ironically, the human night-dream is sometimes closer to the fact of being than are the

---

[109]   Gen. 1:27
[110]   Rom. 13:1
[111]   Heb. 13:8

thoughts of human beings when they are awake. For example, the night-dreams present fewer limitations, less bulk. The dreamer can freely fly through the air.

People are the reflection of Soul, the direct opposite of externalized falsity, and Soul is the one Ego. We run into error when we divide Ego into egos or multiply Mind into minds. Misunderstandings occur when we suppose error to be mind, mind to be in matter and matter to be a lawgiver. We feel stuck between a rock and a hard place when we assume unintelligence is to act like intelligence or that mortality is the matrix of immortality.

Mortal existence is a dream; mortal existence has no real entity, but mimics "I Am." Spirit is the Ego which never dreams, but understands all things. Spiritual Ego never mistakes and is always conscious. Spirit never believes or decides, but knows; Soul is never born and never dies. Spiritual person is the likeness of this Ego. We are not God, but we are the outcome of God. We reflect God.

Fleshly body and mind are of the one and same mortal perception and that one is mistakenly called man and woman. A human being is not God's child, for man and woman are spiritual. Returning to the dream analogy, depending on the dream they entertain, human beings can find themselves tired or in pain, afraid, oblivious to danger, enjoying or suffering. From an observer's point of view, the dreamer's body is just lying there. Of course, when the dreamer wakes, the feelings vanish and the awakened human being is found not at all to be experiencing those dream-sensations.

Is there any more reality in the waking dream of human existence than in the sleeping dream? There can't be, since whatever appears to be a human being is a mortal dream. Take away the mortal human mind and the body doesn't know if it is a person or a tree. The immortal, real person is spiritual.

Human existence is like a soap-opera. The human mind's performance consists of mortal thoughts chasing after each other only to always find disaster and heartache. Conversely, in the theater of divine Science, Life is revealed as not being at the mercy of mortality. Science cannot admit that happiness is ever the sport of circumstance.

Error does not need to demand more and more attention as it accelerates toward self-destruction. For example, concerning what human belief calls an abscess, the sore does not need to become more painful before the pus is absorbed or drained. Or, in the case of a fever, the fever doesn't need to become severe or critical before it ends.

Fear can be so great at certain points, that human thought will automatically be pushed into a new path. If thought took the path of death, mortals wake to the knowledge of two facts: (1) that they are not dead; (2) that they only entered into a different or interim belief. Truth works out the nothingness of error in just these ways. Sickness, as well as sin, is an error that Christ, Truth, alone can destroy.

We must learn how humankind governs the body—whether through faith in hygiene, in drugs, or in will-power. Does humankind govern the body through a belief in the necessity of sickness and death, sin and pardon? Or, does humanity govern it from the higher understanding that the divine Mind makes perfect? Divine Mind acts on the human mind through truth, leading it to relinquish its falsities and find the divine Mind to be the only Mind and the healer of bad-will, syndromes, and fatality. This process of higher spiritual understanding improves humanity until error disappears, and nothing is left which deserves to perish or to be punished.

Lack of immortal awareness, which is identical to intentional wrong, is not Science. Ignorance must be seen and corrected before we can reach harmony. Chaotic and contradictory beliefs commit identity theft, giving matter the identity of Mind. The beliefs also set their own imaginations up as all-important (even as heroes), and thereby isolate themselves to, or confine themselves in, what they create. Beliefs are at war with Science, and as Jesus said, "Every city or household divided against itself will not stand."[112]

Any skepticism in regard to the pathology and theology of divine Science comes from being unfamiliar with Mind. Skepticism is also occasioned by an unawareness of the recuperative energies of Truth.

Knowledge of error and how it operates must precede the understanding of Truth. When false human beliefs learn even a little of their own falsity they begin to disappear. Spiritual understanding then destroys error until the entire human, materialist error finally disappears. The eternal verity, man and woman created by and of Spirit, is understood and recognized as the true likeness of our Maker.

---

[112] Matt. 12:25; Mark 3:24–25; Luke 11:17

The illusive evidence of physical sense certainly differs from the testimony of Spirit. Physical sense lifts its voice with the arrogance of reality and brags, saying: I am completely dishonest, and people don't know it. I can commit adultery, cheat, lie, steal, and murder. I evade detection by pretending to be a victim. My tendency is irrational, my feelings are deceitful, and my purpose is fraudulent, but I aim to make my short span of life one big fling. Resistance to spirituality is fantastic! How it succeeds, where the good purpose waits! The world is my territory. I am popular, surrounded by materialism. However, a reality check, an accident, or the law of God may at any moment annihilate my peace, for all my fancied joys are fatal. Like bursting lava, I increase but to my own despair, because the over-rated mortal human life is a consuming fire.

The testimony of Spirit, Soul, maintains: I am Spirit. Man and woman, whose perceptions are spiritual, are my likeness, reflecting the infinite understanding, for I am Infinity. The beauty of holiness, the perfection of being, and imperishable glory—all are Mine, for I am God. I give spirituality, for I am Truth. I include and impart all happiness, for I am Love. I give life, without beginning and without end, for I am Life. I am supreme, an unlimited source of good ideas, for I am Mind. I am the substance of all, because "I AM WHO I AM."[113]

I hope, dear reader, I am leading you into the understanding of your divine rights, your heaven-bestowed harmony. I hope, as you read, you see there is no cause (outside of imperfect imprints which is not power) able to make you sick, troubled, or sinful. I also hope that you are conquering egocentric thinking. Knowing the illusiveness of limited perceptions, you can assert your prerogative to overcome the belief in a worthless self, in disease, or mortality.

If you believe in and practice wrong knowingly, you can at once change your course and do right. Matter can make no opposition to right endeavors against sin or sickness, for matter can't do anything on its own without mind. If you believe you have a disease, you can alter this wrong belief and action without hindrance from the body.

---

[113] Ex. 3:14

Do not believe in any supposed necessity for failure, adversity, or ruin, knowing (as you ought to know) that God never requires obedience to a physical law because no such law exists. Linear thinking is destroyed by the law of God, which is the law of Life eternal instead of death, of harmony instead of disorder, of Spirit instead of the flesh.

The divine demand, "Be perfect, therefore, as your heavenly Father is perfect,"[114] is scientific, and the human footsteps leading to perfection are requisite. Individuals are consistent, who, watching and praying, can "run and not grow weary . . . walk and not be faint,"[115] who rapidly gain goodness and hold their position, or attain slowly and yield not to discouragement. God requires perfection, but not until the battle between Spirit and flesh is fought and the victory won. To stop eating, drinking, or being clothed materially before the spiritual facts of existence are gained step by step, is not legitimate. When we wait patiently on God and seek Truth righteously, Spirit directs our thought and action. Imperfect human beings grasp the ultimate of spiritual perfection slowly; but to *begin* aright and to continue the strife of demonstrating the great problem of being is doing much.

> Be sensible. Don't try to prove you are some super spiritual human. Eat right, exercise, strive to impact less the body and earth, rest, learn how to communicate with other people, and get help from whoever God leads you to.

During the sensualist age, absolute divine Science may not be achieved prior to the change called death, for we have not the power to demonstrate what we do not understand. The human self must be evangelized. This task God demands us to accept gracefully today, to abandon so fast as practical the temporal, and to work out the spiritual which determines the outward and actual.

---

[114]   Matt. 5:48
[115]   Isa. 40:31

If you float on the quiet surface of error and are in sympathy with error, what is there to disturb the waters? What is there to strip off error's disguise?

If you dare to launch your ship on the ever-agitated but healthful waters of truth, you will encounter storms. The good you do will be spoken of as evil. This is the responsibility. Be accountable. For in answering to Spirit you will win and feel the honor. Stranger on earth, your home is heaven; foreigner, you are the guest of God.

CALLING OUT THE NAYSAYERS

By Cheryl Petersen

When people act on an opportunity, naysayers will show up as spectators and stop at nothing to prevent progress or create a general feeling of confusion in the crowd. But who are the naysayers? Are they hazardous, or do they autodestruct? Is the naysayer outside us, or inside? Naysayers are not people per se but attitudes, sometimes fearful, sometimes sanctimonious, but attitudes not applicable to progress, or the sense of heaven on earth. The definitive answer to naysayers is to love the hell out of them.

Counterintuitive to human reason is the directive to love our enemies the naysayers, an idea that was taught not only by Christ Jesus, but by Buddha, Gandhi, and many other great people and religions. Essentially, the love referred to here doesn't imply forming an alliance or sympathizing with naysayers. On the contrary, this love begins with spiritual Love, it does not begin with the naysayer. When we try to love the naysayer, we give up. However, to love universal Love is to join unbroken progress, a movement that can't be intercepted by pessimism or disapproval. And, by default, the love of Love will ameliorate naysayers (but they will probably deny it).

Evidence has it that progressive opportunities are available for the taking. People who are willing to discover and share forward-movement will seize the opportunities, big or small. Conversely, naysayers refuse to act with progressive ideas mainly because they are relentlessly preoccupied with repeating behavior outgrown by society.

Naysayers will however stray from their isolated lives long enough to give thumbs down to the brave souls willing to follow their inspiration. Quite often, and understandably, the thumbs down are returned with a middle finger up by the brave souls. Or, dejectedly, human bravery gets intimidated and hesitant. However, those reactions are distractions, therefore we take the crucial step of loving infinite Love which in turn bolsters our bravery to act on the inspired idea underlying the opportunity, and furthermore formulate and act on realistic expectations, persistence, and spiritual acumen.

Seriously, human beings are not perfect, but fortunately they can be inspired. Bottom line is: we get pissed; we get stupid; we resent; we talk too much; we delude ourselves; we judge poorly. But then a discovery, or revelation, or epiphany, or knock on the head inspires us to observe, learn, forgive, relate better, share goodness, act on and encourage creative beneficial barrier breaking ideas.

Bear in mind, human beings are notorious for getting a plethora of ideas but some ideas are terrible. So it does help to test the credibility of an idea by bouncing it off other people or even improving the idea before acting on it. This is where level-headedness and honesty come in. Amazingly, level-headedness can even filter practical advice out of a conversation with an authentic naysayer. Likewise, honesty is quick to reject incompetent information that comes from an optimistic expert. But, in general level-headedness and honesty keep the inspired idea in a safe haven of silence and as a result you gain the strength and stamina to move forward.

If circumstances require it, you can confidently call out naysayers by defending, not yourself, but the inspired idea. That is enough. Stay with Love. Naysayer's opinions are self-sabotaging.

Giving birth to an inspired idea exposes naysayers. But because naysayers are always seven steps behind, simply keep looking ahead and moving forward. The naysaying attitude may yell like hell for your attention however in a weird sort of way, naysayers can be seen as a cheering squad, intriguing you to experience infinite Love and its law of progress.

DEBUNKING SOME MISCONCEPTIONS ABOUT *SCIENCE AND HEALTH*

Yet because I tell the truth, you do not believe me! Can any of you prove me guilty of sin? If I am telling the truth, why don't you believe me?[116]

And if the Spirit of him who raised Jesus from the dead is living in you, he who raised Christ from the dead will also give life to your mortal bodies through his Spirit, who lives in you.[117]

To restrict *Science and Health* to any parameter would condemn to oblivion the truth. The truth strengthens the weak and elevates human consciousness from a theoretical to a practical Christianity. Remarks that disapprove of *Science and Health* are generally based on unrelated sentences or phrases separated from their context. Even the Scriptures, which grow in beauty and consistency from one grand root, appear contradictory when torn apart and exposed to such usage. Jesus said, "Blessed are the pure in heart, for they will see God [Truth]."[118]

In divine Science mere opinion is worthless. Paul remarks about "quarreling over opinions."[119] The time has come when proof and

---

116   John 8:45–46
117   Rom. 8:11
118   Matt. 5:8 (Brackets added by Mary Baker Eddy)
119   Rom. 14:1 (NRSV)

demonstration, instead of opinion and dogma, are summoned to the support of spirituality, "making wise the simple."[120] Proof is essential to evaluate properly the subject of Christianity. Spiritual Science is based on divine Principle; demonstrated according to a divine given rule; and subject to proof. The facts are so numerous in support of divine Science, that misrepresentation and denunciation cannot overthrow it.

Regretfully, unwarranted blame aimed toward scientific Mind-healing, or the denial of Truth, produce sad effects on the sick. To find fault with this Science is presumptuous, in the face of Bible history, and defies the direct instruction of Jesus, "Go into all the world and preach the good news to all creation."[121] To this instruction was added the promise that students will drive out evils and heal the sick. Jesus called upon the seventy-two[122] disciples, as well as the twelve, to heal the sick in any town where they should be kindly received.

Sneers at the application of the word *Science* to Christianity cannot prevent Christianity from being scientific. If Godlike Christianity is not scientific, and Science is not of God, then there is no unified law, and truth becomes an accident. Can empirical research confirm the existence of a system that works according to Scripture?

Divine Science awakens the sinner, rehabilitates the self-deceived, and releases from pain the helpless sufferer. Science speaks the words of Truth to those who are lost, and they answer with rejoicing; it causes the deaf to hear, the lame to walk, and the blind to see. Who would be the first to disown the Christ-likeness of good works, when Jesus allegedly said, "By their fruit you will recognize them."?[123]

If Christian Scientists were teaching or practicing pharmaceutics or obstetrics according to the mainstream medical theories, little denunciation would follow them even if their treatment resulted in the death of a patient. The people are taught in such cases to say, it was God's will. Why then, am I maligned for healing, for teaching Truth as the Principle of healing, and for proving my word by my deed? James said: "Show me your faith without deeds, and I will show you my faith by what I do."[124]

---

[120]   Ps. 19:7
[121]   Mark 16:15
[122]   Some documents say, seventy
[123]   Matt. 7:20
[124]   James 2:18

Isn't the human mind unaware of God's methods? This makes it doubly unfair for human beings to impugn and misrepresent the spiritual facts. In regard to the human mind's misrepresentations of God, eventually a person is able to say, "None of these things move me."[125] It is enlightened sense that understands God. Even though Truth is unjustly distorted, it will not forever be hidden from the enlightened sense of the people. The sick, the disabled, and the blind look to divine Science and receive blessing.

Jesus strips all disguise from error when his teachings are fully understood. By parable and argument he explains the impossibility of good producing evil. Jesus also scientifically demonstrates the allness of good, proving by what are wrongly called miracles, that sin, sickness, and death are beliefs—illusive errors—which he could and did destroy.

It would sometimes seem as if truth were rejected because humility and spirituality are the conditions of its acceptance, while Christendom generally demands so much less.

The apostles who were Jesus' students, as well as Paul who was not his student, healed the sick and reformed the sinner by means of spirituality. The common human mistakes are to assume spiritual advancement is dependent on a religious organization, and to assume we can follow Jesus' and Paul's examples with words rather than works. Whoever is first, humbly and conscientiously, to press along the line of gospel-healing, is considered a heretic.

Christian Science is sometimes disapproved of because it claims God as the only absolute Life and Soul, and man and woman to be God's idea—that is, Spirit's image. However, Scriptures confirm the claim, saying that God created "man" (a generic term for man and woman given in many Bible versions), "in our image, in our likeness."[126] Is it sacrilegious to assume that God's likeness is not found in fleshly beings, sin, sickness, and death? In reality, the person referred to as God's image represents the normal, healthful, and sinless condition of man and woman in divine Science.

Truth heals and error causes disease. If that action were understood, people who deny a demonstrable Science would perhaps mercifully

---

[125]   Acts 20:24 (KJV)
[126]   Gen. 1:26

withhold their misrepresentations which harm the sick. Until the opponents of divine Science test its efficacy according to its rules which reveal its usefulness or uselessness, it would be fair to observe the Scriptural precept, "Do not judge."[127]

Complementary and alternative medicines (CAM), osteopathy, chiropractics, and conventional medicine are employed to treat disease. However, Jesus did not need any of these methods. The divine Science which he preached and practiced certainly healed and it should be presented to the whole world.

Why would a person refuse to investigate Jesus' method of treating disease when it was shown to work? Why default to the conventional mainstream systems when surgeries, harmful drug reactions, and substance abuse cause a number of complications? Is it because health insurance pays for those systems? Is it because orthodoxy is more fashionable?

In the Bible the word *Spirit* is so commonly applied to Deity that Spirit and God are often regarded as synonymous terms; and Spirit is exactly how God is understood in Christian Science. It is evident that the likeness of Spirit can't be material, therefore, doesn't it follow that God can't be in Spirit's unlikeness and work through matter to heal the sick? When the omnipotence of God is preached and Spirit's absoluteness is conveyed, the sick will be healed.

In his book, *Healing and Christianity*, Morton Kelsey presents a history of healing in the Christian church, pointing out the tendency of our culture to ignore the possibility of healing through divine intervention. Kelsey explains that divine intervention is often disregarded by theology and philosophy because the connection between religion and healing is difficult to explain. Some students of theology and philosophy may even criticize religious leaders who heal through Christ, Truth, in order to cover up their own lack of healing ability. Kelsey states, "There are some who, on the side, poke fun at the theological vagaries of Mary Baker Eddy."[128] A person who understands divine Science can heal the sick via divine Principle, and this practical proof is the only feasible evidence that one does understand this Science well enough to pass judgment on it. The theology of divine Science, including Christian healing, is consistent. In

---

127   Matt. 7:1; Luke 6:37; John 7:24
128   Kelsey, Morton T. *Healing and Christianity.* New York: Harper & Row, 1973.

this volume there are no contradictory statements apparent to those who understand its propositions.

When we are able to perceive the inconsistency between mortal human beings and God's idea, we can discern the distinction (made by Science) between human mortal persons and God's spiritual person, made in Spirit's image.

The apostle says: "For if those who are nothing think they are something, they deceive themselves."[129] The thought of human material nothingness (which Science urges) enrages the human ego and is the main cause of its resistance to new ideas.

The distinction needs to be clear between God's idea as the ideal person, and the human's idea of person. There is no perfect mortal human. In order to achieve the ideal of God, you must be careful not to fall into the human mind's tendency to believe that a particular human routine or lifestyle will guarantee spirituality. To insist on a particular human way of life as a means of achieving perfection, doesn't achieve God's ideal. For example, someone who thinks, "We do not seek sex; we do not try drugs; we do not take medicine; we do not go to doctors,"[130] will be disappointed in divine Science. To avoid sex, drugs, medicine, and doctors, is the same as robotically having sex, taking drugs, and going to a doctor. Neither are a means of reaching the spiritual ideal. The imperative point is to understand God's ideal and let the divine understanding impel your thoughts and actions as a part of humanity. Our ideal directs our lifestyles, not vice versa. The teachings found in *Science and Health* uncover spirituality, the understanding of God's ideal.

Thought must stay open to metaphysical ideas in science, theology, and medicine. Thought cannot obsess or fixate on lifestyles, symbols, or a favorite rule; otherwise people will lose touch with reason and develop a narrow and blurred view of reality—they will make mistakes, errors. Consider a successful math student. The student can't focus on only the rule of addition when working out a problem that also involves subtraction or division. Fixations cause not only confusion, but also the penchant to guess and a lack of mental improvement.

---

[129]   Gal. 6:3 (NRSV)
[130]   *The Unseen Shore* by Thomas Simmons. Copyright © 1991 by Thomas Simmons. Reprinted by permission of Beacon Press, Boston.

We must be open to all of the principles in Science and they need to be learned and applied in life's situations, otherwise error will be an unbroken head-wind.

Some critics think that Christian Scientists are deluded, or in some vacuum, because error is revealed as unreal. For instance, a Christian apologist, attempting to interpret the teachings of Christian Science, says of Christian Scientists, "Their religious worldview teaches that sickness and pain are an illusion; they do not exist. But this belief is valid only by rejecting the fact that truth corresponds to reality."[131] The fact that truth corresponds to reality is not rejected in Christian Science. Instead, Christian Science reveals that much of the reality before the human perceptions is not actually true, for example the earth isn't a motionless solid mass but consists of forces in constant motion. Truth, reality, has no error; therefore disbelief in error destroys error and leads to discernment of Truth.

We treat error through the understanding of Truth, because Truth is error's antidote. Error is like a dream, and when a dream stops, it is self-destroyed and the terror is over. Take pain. Many times over, pain disappears as dreams do. It may seem absurd to say pain is an illusion (dream), however, what else could it be? Human beings have forever been at odds when measuring pain levels. A painful condition to one person isn't even noticed by another person. More bizarre is the fact that pain to one human being is actually pleasure to another. Pain has even been proven to be an error on the physical level. When a supposedly pained human mind is distracted, unconscious, or drugged, where is the pain? Pain is an error, sometimes a terror. Error has no part of Truth and this is an antidote that removes any terror.

Superstitions and a lack of knowledge within your own human framework must be expelled to make room for spiritual understanding. We cannot serve both the human and divine framework at the same time; but isn't this what frail mortals are trying to do? Paul says: "For the sinful nature desires what is contrary to the Spirit, and the Spirit what is contrary to the sinful nature."[132] Are you ready to admit this?

---

[131]   Taken from *Christianity on the Offense: Responding to the Beliefs and Assumptions of Spiritual Seeker* © 1998 by Dan Story. Published by Kregel Publications, Grand Rapids, MI. Used by permission of the publisher. All rights reserved.

[132]   Gal. 5:17

Critics who attack faith should be careful not to confuse spiritual faith with blind faith. Faith is necessary in science, medicine, and religion. Consider the researcher or scientist who is trying to find a cure for cancer; they obviously have faith that a cure exists; otherwise they would not even try. People who cannot distinguish between blind (ritualistic) faith and that of spiritual faith are easily misinformed. They can make irrational, unfortunate statements such as: "If your beliefs are those of a Christian Scientist, obliging you to forgo all medical interventions, you may even have collaborated with God by refusing to give your child antibiotics."[133] Christian Science does not "oblige" any particular human action as if people are androids. A student of Christian Science does not collaborate with God as if God is a separate mind. In Science, there is no attitude of give-and-take; there is no human element that says, "If you do this, I'll do that." Do physicists collaborate with the law of gravity in order to go to the moon? No. Scientists study the principles of physics, they have the faith those rules will work, they apply the principles, and they go to the moon. Comments and condemnations based on a lack of research are embarrassing to the critic and obscure any good points being made.

Opponents should consider that the mortal human being is not the reality of God's child, and this consideration will allow the mind to receive new ideas that lead to progress and well-being, to receive epiphanies, if you will, as a result of Christ in action. The Christ-spirit comes now as of old, preaching the good news to receptive minds, healing the sick, and destroying evils. Can error, human intellect, or any human invention, restore the essential element of spirituality—namely, apostolic, divine healing? No, the Science of Christ is restoring it, and is the light shining in darkness, a darkness that does not overcome the light.

If divine Science takes away the popular gods—sin, sickness, and death—it is Christ, Truth, who destroys these evils, and so proves their nothingness.

The dream that human mind and error are real or permanent must yield to reason and enlightenment. Then human beings will perceive the insubstantiality of sin and sickness, and sin and sickness will disappear from consciousness. The harmonious will appear real and

---

133   Harris, Sam. *The End of Faith*. New York: W. W. Norton & Company, 2005.

the inharmonious will become extinct. Erroneous perceptions are seen as false gods, nonbeings; gods we do not desire to honor or fear.

When the medical field finds no biological or physical cause for symptoms of disease, various forms of psychotherapy have been known to improve the unhealthy condition. Psychosomatic illnesses or psychophysiological disorders are admitted to be problems caused by mental processes. They are problems in the mind, and once the mind is corrected, the symptoms vanish as illusions vanish. Mental conditions, such as severe stress, anger, anxiety, resentment, depression, and guilt have produced rashes, allergies, loss of hair, eating disorders, and pain, among other problems. So, why not approve of a cure which in effect makes any disease appear to be what it really is—an illusion?

Here is the difficulty: it is not generally understood how one disease can be just as much a delusion as another. It is a pity that the medical faculty and clergy have not learned this, for Jesus established this fundamental fact when devils (delusions) were driven to oblivion and the mute spoke.

Are we irreverent toward sin, or assigning too much power to God, when we ascribe to Him almighty Life and Love? I deny God's cooperation with evil and desire to have no faith in evil or in any power but God, good. Isn't it better to eliminate from so-called human mind that which, so long as it remains in human mind, will show itself in forms of sin, sickness, and death? Why complain of suffering while at the same time tenaciously defending the rights of disease? Wouldn't it be better to abandon the defense, especially when by doing so our own condition can be improved and that of other persons as well?

I have never supposed the world would immediately leave everything for divine Science, or that people would instantly stop believing in sin, disease, and death. However, I do state that, as a result of teaching Christian Science, ethics and moderation have received a stimulus, health has been restored, and people are living longer. If that was the fruit of the turn of the 20th century, what will the harvest be, when this Science is more generally understood?

Paul asked the megalomaniacal leaders the same question we ask today concerning healing and teaching, "You who brag about the law, do you dishonor God by breaking the law?"[134] Jesus annulled fleshly

---

[134] Rom. 2:23

law by healing contrary to those human laws. We have the gospel. We propose to follow Jesus' model, by obeying spiritual law which can overcome material law. Two essential points of Truth's law are that Life and spiritual being do not die, and God is not the author of sickness.

The major obstacle in conveying the teachings of divine Science accurately to human thought is that English, like all other languages, is inadequate to express spiritual concepts and intents. We have to use incomplete terms and symbols in dealing with spiritual ideas. The elucidation of Mind-science resides in its spiritual sense, and students need first to recognize their spiritual senses in order to grasp the meaning of divine Science. Out of this condition grew the prophecy concerning the apostles, "They will speak in new tongues."[135]

While dwelling on a physical plane, human terms must generally be employed to speak of the things of Spirit. It takes time for human thought to adjust to the higher meaning. Thought must be educated to perceive spirituality. To a certain extent, improved thought is necessary in all learning, even in that which is secular.

In divine Science, substance is understood to be Mind, while the disputer of Christian Science believes substance to be human mind and material things. Disputers believe the human mind and its projections are almost the only substance, and that the things which pertain to Spirit are next to nothing, or are very far removed from daily experience.

To understand all of Jesus' sayings as recorded in the New Testament, followers must advance into that stature of selfhood in Christ Jesus which enables them to interpret the ongoing vital spiritual meaning. Spiritual understanding knows how Truth dissolves error and heals the sick. Jesus' words were the offspring of his deeds, both of which must be understood. Unless the works are comprehended which his words explained, the words are blind.

Jesus often refused to explain his words. He said: "For this people's heart has become calloused; they hardly hear with their ears, and they have closed their eyes. Otherwise they might see with their eyes, hear with their ears, understand with their hearts and turn, and I would heal them."[136] The materialist milieu has a difficult time understanding spiritual Truth.

---

[135] Mark 16:17
[136] Isa. 6:10; Matt. 13:15; Acts 28:27

"The Word became flesh."[137] Truth must be known by its effects on the body as well as on the human mind before the Science of being can be demonstrated. The idea of the Word becoming flesh was embodied in the incarnate Jesus. He was a life-link forming the connection through which the real reaches the unreal; through which Soul rebukes mortal impressions; and Truth destroys error.

If the Word is explained through mortal convictions, the spiritual meaning will scarcely be perceived. Religion which stems from half-hidden history is pretentious and void of healing power. When we lose faith in God's power to heal or distrust the Principle of divine Science, we will project the belief that it is impossible to heal spiritually. It is difficult to heal metaphysically if we position ourselves on a material basis.

I became a member of the orthodox Congregational Church in early years. Later in life, I learned that my own prayers failed to heal me as did the prayers of my devout parents and the church. However, when the spiritual view of religion was discerned in Science, this view was a present help. The spiritual sense is the living, pulsating presence of Christ, Truth, which healed, and heals, the sick.

We can't bring out the practical proof of spirituality which Jesus required while error seems as potent and real to us as Truth. We can't make a personal devil and an anthropomorphic God our starting points—especially if we consider Satan as a being coequal in power with, or superior to, the Almighty. Such starting points are neither spiritual nor scientific and they can't work out the metaphysical principles of divine healing, which prove the nothingness of error by demonstrating the all-inclusiveness of harmonious Truth.

Some worshipper's center thought on the material in an attempt to worship the spiritual. To these worshippers, the human perceptions, rituals, and worldly ways and means are substance and Spirit is insubstantial. But it is impossible to worship Spirit from the incongruous standpoint of human reverences and agendas. The people might appeal to their personal concepts or false gods, but their prayer brings no proof that it was heard, because they did not sufficiently understand God to be able to demonstrate His power to heal—to make harmony the reality and disorder the unreality.

---

[137] John 1:14

Jesus was known to say that his fleshly body was not spirit, evidently considering it a human and changeable belief of flesh and bones. People, even the religious leaders, did not share his view because the spiritual was the intangible and uncertain, if not the unreal.

Would a parent say to a child who is frightened by ghosts or sickened by fear of ghosts, "I know that ghosts are real. Ghosts exist and are to be feared, but you must not be afraid of them"?

It is absurd for children, or adults, to pretend not to be afraid of something scary. We have to understand the unreality of what scares us, otherwise, at any moment we may become a helpless victim. However, instead of increasing fears by declaring a bogeyman, or animal magnetism, or disease, to be real, merciless, and powerful, thus watering the very roots of helpless timidity, we should gain the spiritual understanding that assures us fear is groundless because ghosts and diseases are not realities, but are only a downward spiraling imagination, erroneous and human-made.

Tell children not to believe in ghosts and explain the good that is worthy of respect and honor. If you destroy the thinking that ghosts are real, terror from the ghosts will fade and health will be restored. Objects of alarm will vanish and no longer seem worthy of fear or honor. To accomplish a good result, it is certainly not irrational to tell the truth about ghosts.

The spiritually scientific real goes unnoticed by the physical nervous system and cognitive ability. Likewise, negativity, confusion, erratic love/hate relationships, loss, whatever seems real to fleshly sense, is unreal in divine Science. The physical senses and Science have ever been antagonistic, and they will so continue until the physical senses entirely yield to scientific spirituality.

How can a person, who has glimpsed the evidence of Truth, any longer believe in the reality of error, either in the form of sickness or sin? All must admit that Christ, Truth, is "the way and the truth and the life,"[138] and that omnipotent Truth certainly does destroy error.

Human minds have not completely outgrown their superstitions. Human mindsets embody ghostly beliefs, and time is required before reaching eternity, spirituality, or complete reality. All the real is eternal. Perfection underlies reality. Without perfection, nothing is completely

---

[138] John 14:6

real. Temporal things will continue to be outgrown until perfection appears and reality is reached. Old-wives-tales, even new old-wives tales, need to become a thing of the past. We must not continue to be impressed by superstitious thinking, but we must be wise and let go of all misdirected reverences. When we learn that error is not real, we are ready for progress, "forgetting what is behind."[139]

Death will not banish the virtual reality of mortal existence. False perceptions and superstitions persist when humans limit Mind. Mind is limitless. Mind never was limited. The true idea of being is spiritual and immortal, and from this it follows that whatever is not of immortality is unreal. Human beliefs cannot demonstrate spirituality or comprehend the reality of Life.

The teachings of Christian Science are grounded in Scripture, but yet critics warn people, "of its teachings which are in dire contradiction to the Word of God."[140] To obey Scripture is to heal as Jesus healed, divinely. Why deny Christian Science, when it teaches divine healing? The words of divine Science find their immortality in deeds, for their Principle heals the sick and spiritualizes humanity.

Opponents of Christian Science neither give nor offer any proof that their Master's religion can heal the sick. Surely we need to do more than preserve unreliable and useless dogmas, derived from religious traditions and stamped with human approval or authorization.

Inconsistency is shown by words without deeds, which is like a car without an engine. If our words fail to express our deeds, God will redeem that weakness and out of the mouth of babes Soul will perfect praise. Consistency is seen in example more than in precept. The night of materiality is burning out, and Truth's glow wakens human beings spiritually to hear and to speak the new tongue.

Wrongdoing should become unreal to everyone. Sin is inconsistent, a divided kingdom with a realism that has no divine authority, and I rejoice in the understanding of this grand truth.

The opponents of divine Science must be charitable if they would be Christian. If the letter of divine Science appears inconsistent, gain the spiritual meaning of Mind-science and the ambiguity will vanish.

---

[139] Phil. 3:13
[140] Robinson, Dean. *The Anit-Christian Unscientific Cult.* http://www.tbaptist.com/aab/christianscience.htm Accessed 10/01/2006.

The charge of inconsistency in Christ-like scientific methods of dealing with disease is rendered pointless by the proof of the utility of these methods. Proofs are better than verbal arguments—better than prayers which don't manifest the spiritual power to heal.

As for sickness and unprogressive mindsets, divine Science says in the language of the Teacher, "Follow me, and let the dead bury their own dead."[141] In other words, let disorder of every name and nature be heard no more, and let the harmonious and true sense of Life and being occupy human consciousness.

There are two conflicting theories regarding Christian healing. One, according to the commands of Jesus, heals the sick now. The other, taught by mainstream religion, professes that Christian healing hasn't happened since the first century. What is the relative value of these differing theories?

Some people condemn Christian Science because *Science and Health* refers to God as Principle. Misleading comments are made such as, "It is therefore important to remember that Eddy never believed in a personal God nor does any true Christian Scientist today."[142] God doesn't have a human personality but is the One Person, reflected uniquely by individual ideas, therefore, a very close personal relationship can be felt. Our personal relationship with Principle is higher and grander than human mortal friendship, which requires something outside ourselves and is often selective or exclusive.

Strangely enough, we ask for physical theories to support spiritual and eternal truths, when the two are so antagonistic that the materialist thought must become spiritualized before the spiritual fact is attained. The material existence affords no evidence of spiritual being or immortality. Sin, sickness, and death do not prove the immortality of person. Discord can never establish the facts of harmony. Matter is not the threshold of Spirit.

Jesus reasoned practically on the subject of existence, controlling sickness, sin, and death on the grounds of spiritual existence. Understanding the insubstantiality of material things, he spoke of the flesh and Spirit as two opposites—as error and Truth, not contributing

141 Matt. 8:22; Luke 9:60
142 Martin, Walter, and Zacharias, Ravi, *The Kingdom of the Cults,* Revised and Updated and Expanded Edition. Minnesota: Bethany House, 2003.

in any way to each other's happiness and being. It has been recorded that Jesus said, "The Spirit gives life; the flesh counts for nothing."[143]

There is no immediate or on-going partnership between error and Truth, between flesh and Spirit. God is as incapable of producing wickedness, sickness, and mortality as Truth is of experiencing these errors. How then is it possible for Mind to create spiritual being, made in the divine likeness, capable of experiencing that which is unlike the divine?

Does evil proceed from good? Does God create a human out of Spirit? Does divine Love commit fraud by making man and woman free to do wrong, and then stand on the sidelines to punish the wrongdoer? Would anyone call it wise and good for God to create people and then condemn them to remain His enemy, prisoner, or an orphan?

Subsequent follows its precedent. An intelligent sinless God precedes an intelligent sinless creation. God did not create sin and sin can't be self-creative, because God is the only Creator. There is not a second creator making people who need to be corrected.

God's "eyes are too pure to look on evil."[144] Truth is sustained, not by accepting, but by rejecting a lie.

Jesus was quoted to define anthropomorphic evil as, "a liar and the father of lies."[145] Truth does not materialize a lie, a capacity to lie, or a liar. If humankind would stop believing that God makes sickness, destruction, and death, or makes man and woman capable of suffering on account of this malevolence, the games of error would no longer be played and error's destruction would be guaranteed. Seriously, if we accept that disease and destruction are God's will, why do we try to fight or avoid disease and destruction? God isn't testing us, because God's will is good and can only produce goodness.

Looking back at history, we can learn that the popular and misleading perceptions about the divine Being and character have originated in the human mind. Wrong notions about God do not originate in immortal Truth. As there is in reality but one God, one Mind, mistaken impressions of God eventually fade out according to the vision of St. John in Revelation.

---

[143]   John 6:63
[144]   Hab. 1:13
[145]   John 8:44

If that which contradicts God is real, there must be two powers and then God would not be powerful and infinite. Can the Higher Power be Almighty if another mighty and self-creative cause exists and influences humankind? If the divine Parent has "Life in himself,"[146] as Scriptures say, could Life, or God, live in evil and create it? Can matter control Life, Spirit, therefore, and so defeat omnipotence?

Is the chainsaw, which destroys a tree's so-called life, superior to omnipotence? Can a bullet deprive consciousness of Life—that is, of God, who is the life of spiritual being? Clinically dead people have returned to life and said they still had a consciousness. God, Life, is not at the mercy of matter/energy. The doctrine that matter has power is "confusion worse confounded."[147] If two statements directly contradict each other and one is true, the other must be false. Is Science therefore contradictory?

Divine Science, understood, coincides with the Scriptures and sustains logically and demonstratively every point it presents, otherwise it would not be Science and could not present results. Mind-science is not made up of paradoxical clichés or of the inventions of those who ridicule God. Science presents the calm and clear verdict of Truth against error, voiced and illustrated by the prophets, by Jesus, and by his apostles—as recorded throughout Scripture.

Why are the words of Jesus more frequently cited for our instruction than his remarkable works? Is it because not many people know how important those works are to spirituality?

Is it likely that some people have more faith in a Christian Scientist, whom they have perhaps never seen and against whom they have been warned, than they have in their own accredited and orthodox leaders, whom they have seen and have been taught to love and to trust?

Let a member of the clergy try to cure a friend through personal faith in the clergy. Will that faith heal them? Yet Scientists will take the same case and cures can follow. Faith must be in God. I have healed unbelievers whose only objection to this method was, that I as a Christian Scientist believed in the Holy Spirit, while they, the patient, did not.

---

[146]   John 5:26
[147]   Milton, John, (1608–1974) *Paradise Lost.* Book 2, line 996.

Even though you insist that the physical senses are indispensable to your existence or entity, you must change the human concept of life, and must extensively know yourself spiritually and scientifically. The evidence of the existence of Spirit, Soul, is substantial only to spiritual sense. Manifest Soul is not apparent to the limited senses—senses which cognize only that which opposes Spirit.

True spirituality is to be honored wherever found, but when will we arrive at the goal which that word implies? From Puritan parents, I received my religious education. In childhood, I often listened with joy to these words falling from the lips of my saintly mother, "God is able to raise you up from sickness." I pondered the meaning of the Scripture: "And these signs will accompany those who believe: . . . they will place their hands on sick people and they will get well."[148]

A student of spiritual Science and a student of physical science are like two different artists. One says: "I have spiritual ideals, indestructible and glorious. When others see them as I do, in their true light and loveliness—and know that these ideals are real and eternal because drawn from Truth—they will find that nothing is lost and all is won, by a correct estimate of what is real."

The other artist replies: "You flaw my experience. My mind-ideals are both mental and material. It is true that materialization renders these ideals imperfect and destructible; yet I would not exchange mine for yours, for mine give me instant self-gratification, and they are not so shockingly transcendental. They don't require me to be unselfish. They keep Soul well out of sight. Moreover, I have no notion of losing my old doctrines or human opinions."

Now then reader, which mind-picture or expressed thought will be real to you—the spiritual or the temporal? Both you cannot have. You are bringing out your own ideal. This ideal is either eternal or temporal. Either Spirit or matter is your model. If you try to have two models, then you practically have none. Like a yo-yo, you will spin and bounce between the unreal and the real.

Hear the wisdom of Job—

Can mortals be righteous before God?

Can human beings be pure before their Maker?

Even in his servants he puts no trust,

---

[148]   Mark 16:17–18

And his angels he charges with error.[149]

Jesus was put to death for the truth he spoke and demonstrated. Today, there is interfaith dialogue and divine Science mediates to explain differing doctrinal points, cancel disagreements, and settle questions. Jew and Christian can unite in doctrine and denomination on the very basis of Jesus' words and works. The Jew believes that the Messiah or Christ has not yet come; the Christian believes that Christ is God. Christ isn't God. Christ, as the true spiritual idea, is the ideal of God now and forever, here and everywhere. The Jew and Christian can unite on the doctrine that God is One and is present now and forever. It is recognizable that Jesus Christ is not God, as Jesus himself declared, but is the Son of God. This fact understood, doesn't conflict with another statement: "I and the Father are one"[150]—because Christ and God are one in quality, not in quantity. As a drop of water is one with the ocean, a ray of light one with the sun, even so God and spiritual being, Parent and child, are one in being. The Scripture reads: "For in him we live and move and have our being."[151]

I have revised *Science and Health* only to give a clearer and fuller expression of its original meaning. Spiritual ideas unfold as we advance. A human perception of divine Science, however limited, must be correct in order to be Science and subject to demonstration. A germ of infinite Truth, though least in the realm of heaven, is the higher hope on earth, but it will be rejected and hated until God prepares the soil for the seed. That which when sown produces immortal fruit, perfects humanity only when it is understood—consequently, the many readings given the Scriptures, and the requisite revisions of *Science and Health with Key to the Scriptures.*

---

[149] Job 4:17–18 (MRSV)
[150] John 10:30
[151] Act. 17:28

Parallel Chapter from Mary Baker Eddy's *Science and Health* with *Key to the Scriptures*

CHAPTER III—MARRIAGE

What therefore God hath joined together, let not man put asunder. In the resurrection they neither marry, nor are given in marriage, but are as the angels of God in heaven.—JESUS.

When our great Teacher came to him for baptism, John was astounded. Reading his thoughts, Jesus added: "Suffer it to be so now: for thus it becometh us to fulfil all righteousness." Jesus' concessions (in certain cases) to material methods were for the advancement of spiritual good.

Marriage is the legal and moral provision for generation among human kind. Until the spiritual creation is discerned intact, is apprehended and understood, and His kingdom is come as in the vision of the Apocalypse,—where the corporeal sense of creation was cast out, and its spiritual sense was revealed from heaven,—marriage will continue, subject to such moral regulations as will secure increasing virtue.

Infidelity to the marriage covenant is the social scourge of all races, "the pestilence that walketh in darkness, the destruction that wasteth at noonday." The commandment, "Thou shalt not commit adultery," is no less imperative than the one, "Thou shalt not kill."

Chastity is the cement of civilization and progress. Without it there is no stability in society, and without it one cannot attain the Science of Life.

Union of the masculine and feminine qualities constitutes completeness. The masculine mind reaches a higher tone through certain elements of the feminine, while the feminine mind gains courage and strength through masculine qualities. These different elements conjoin naturally with each other, and their true harmony is in spiritual oneness. Both sexes should be loving, pure, tender, and strong. The attraction between native qualities will be perpetual only as it is pure and true, bringing sweet seasons of renewal like the returning spring.

Beauty, wealth, or fame is incompetent to meet the demands of the affections, and should never weigh against the better claims of intellect, goodness, and virtue. Happiness is spiritual, born of Truth and Love. It is unselfish; therefore it cannot exist alone, but requires all mankind to share it.

Human affection is not poured forth vainly, even though it meet no return. Love enriches the nature, enlarging, purifying, and elevating it. The wintry blasts of earth may uproot the flowers of affection, and scatter them to the winds; but this severance of fleshly ties serves to unite thought more closely to God, for Love supports the struggling heart until it ceases to sigh over the world and begins to unfold its wings for heaven.

Marriage is unblest or blest, according to the disappointments it involves or the hopes it fulfils. To happify existence by constant intercourse with those adapted to elevate it, should be the motive of society. Unity of spirit gives new pinions to joy, or else joy's drooping wings trail in dust.

Ill-arranged notes produce discord. Tones of the human mind may be different, but they should be concordant in order to blend properly. Unselfish ambition, noble life-motives, and purity,—these constituents of thought, mingling, constitute individually and collectively true happiness, strength, and permanence.

There is moral freedom in Soul. Never contract the horizon of a worthy outlook by the selfish exaction of all another's time and thoughts. With additional joys, benevolence should grow more diffusive. The narrowness and jealousy, which would confine a wife or a husband forever within four walls, will not promote the sweet interchange of confidence and love; but on the other hand, a wandering desire for incessant amusement outside the home circle is a poor augury for the happiness of wedlock. Home is the dearest spot on earth, and it should be the centre, though not the boundary, of the affections.

Said the peasant bride to her lover: "Two eat no more together than they eat separately." This is a hint that a wife ought not to court vulgar extravagance or stupid ease, because another supplies her wants. Wealth may obviate the necessity for toil or the chance for ill-nature in the marriage relation, but nothing can abolish the cares of marriage.

"She that is married careth . . . how she may please her husband," says the Bible; and this is the pleasantest thing to do. Matrimony should never be entered into without a full recognition of its enduring obligations on both sides. There should be the most tender solicitude for each other's happiness, and mutual attention and approbation should wait on all the years of married life.

Mutual compromises will often maintain a compact which might otherwise become unbearable. Man should not be required to participate in all the annoyances and cares of domestic economy, nor should woman be expected to understand political economy. Fulfilling the different demands of their united spheres, their sympathies should blend in sweet confidence and cheer, each partner sustaining the other,—thus hallowing the union of interests and affections, in which the heart finds peace and home.

Tender words and unselfish care in what promotes the welfare and happiness of your wife will prove more salutary in prolonging her health and smiles than stolid indifference or jealousy. Husbands, hear this and remember how slight a word or deed may renew the old trysting-times.

After marriage, it is too late to grumble over incompatibility of disposition. A mutual understanding should exist before this union and continue ever after, for deception is fatal to happiness.

The nuptial vow should never be annulled, so long as its moral obligations are kept intact; but the frequency of divorce shows that the sacredness of this relationship is losing its influence, and that fatal mistakes are undermining its foundations. Separation never should take place, and it never would, if both husband and wife were genuine Christian Scientists. Science inevitably lifts one's being higher in the scale of harmony and happiness.

Kindred tastes, motives, and aspirations are necessary to the formation of a happy and permanent companionship. The beautiful in character is also the good, welding indissolubly the links of affection. A mother's affection cannot be weaned from her child, because the mother-love includes purity and constancy, both of which are immortal. Therefore maternal affection lives on under whatever difficulties.

From the logic of events we learn that selfishness and impurity alone are fleeting, and that wisdom will ultimately put asunder what she hath not joined together.

Marriage should improve the human species, becoming a barrier against vice, a protection to woman, strength to man, and a centre for the affections. This, however, in a majority of cases, is not its present tendency, and why? Because the education of the higher nature is neglected, and other considerations,—passion, frivolous amusements, personal adornment, display, and pride,—occupy thought.

An ill-attuned ear calls discord harmony, not appreciating concord. So physical sense, not discerning the true happiness of being, places it on a false basis. Science will correct the discord, and teach us life's sweeter harmonies.

Soul has infinite resources with which to bless mankind, and happiness would be more readily attained and would be more secure in our keeping, if sought in Soul. Higher enjoyments alone can satisfy the cravings of immortal man. We cannot circumscribe happiness within the limits of personal sense. The senses confer no real enjoyment.

The good in human affections must have ascendency over the evil and the spiritual over the animal, or happiness will never be won. The attainment of this celestial condition would improve our progeny, diminish crime, and give higher aims to ambition. Every valley of sin must be exalted, and every mountain of selfishness be brought low, that the highway of our God may be prepared in Science. The offspring of heavenly-minded parents inherit more intellect, better balanced minds, and sounder constitutions.

If some fortuitous circumstance places promising children in the arms of gross parents, often these beautiful children early droop and die, like tropical flowers born amid Alpine snows. If perchance they live to become parents in their turn, they may reproduce in their own helpless little ones the grosser traits of their ancestors. What hope of happiness, what noble ambition, can inspire the child who inherits propensities that must either be overcome or reduce him to a loathsome wreck?

Is not the propagation of the human species a greater responsibility, a more solemn charge, than the culture of your garden or the raising of stock to increase your flocks and herds? Nothing unworthy of perpetuity should be transmitted to children.

The formation of mortals must greatly improve to advance mankind. The scientific *morale* of marriage is spiritual unity. If the propagation of a higher human species is requisite to reach this goal, then its material conditions can only be permitted for the purpose of generating. The foetus must be kept mentally pure and the period of gestation have the sanctity of virginity.

The entire education of children should be such as to form habits of obedience to the moral and spiritual law, with which the child can meet and master the belief in so-called physical laws, a belief which breeds disease.

If parents create in their babes a desire for incessant amusement, to be always fed, rocked, tossed, or talked to, those parents should not, in after years, complain of their children's fretfulness or frivolity, which the parents themselves have occasioned. Taking less "thought for your life, what ye shall eat, or what ye shall drink"; less thought "for your body what ye shall put on," will do much more for the health of the rising generation than you dream. Children should be allowed to remain children in knowledge, and should become men and women only through growth in the understanding of man's higher nature.

We must not attribute more and more intelligence to matter, but less and less, if we would be wise and healthy. The divine Mind, which forms the bud and blossom, will care for the human body, even as it clothes the lily; but let no mortal interfere with God's government by thrusting in the laws of erring, human concepts.

The higher nature of man is not governed by the lower; if it were, the order of wisdom would be reversed. Our false views of life hide eternal harmony, and produce the ills of which we complain. Because mortals believe in material laws and reject the Science of Mind, this does not make materiality first and the superior law of Soul last. You would never think that flannel was better for warding off pulmonary disease than the controlling Mind, if you understood the Science of being.

In Science man is the offspring of Spirit. The beautiful, good, and pure constitute his ancestry. His origin is not, like that of mortals, in brute instinct, nor does he pass through material conditions prior to reaching intelligence. Spirit is his primitive and ultimate source of being; God is his Father, and Life is the law of his being.

Civil law establishes very unfair differences between the rights of the two sexes. Christian Science furnishes no precedent for such injustice, and civilization mitigates it in some measure. Still, it is a marvel why usage should accord woman less rights than does either Christian Science or civilization.

Our laws are not impartial, to say the least, in their discrimination as to the person, property, and parental claims of the two sexes. If the elective franchise for women will remedy the evil without encouraging difficulties of greater magnitude, let us hope it will be granted. A feasible as well as rational means of improvement at present is the elevation of society in general and the achievement of a nobler race for legislation,—a race having higher aims and motives.

If a dissolute husband deserts his wife, certainly the wronged, and perchance impoverished, woman should be allowed to collect her own wages, enter into business agreements, hold real estate, deposit funds, and own her children free from interference.

Want of uniform justice is a crying evil caused by the selfishness and inhumanity of man. Our forefathers exercised their faith in the direction taught by the Apostle James, when he said: "Pure religion and undefiled before God and the Father, is this, To visit the fatherless and widows in their affliction, and to keep himself unspotted from the world."

Pride, envy, or jealousy seems on most occasions to be the master of ceremonies, ruling out primitive Christianity. When a man lends a helping hand to some noble woman, struggling alone with adversity, his wife should not say, "It is never well to interfere with your neighbor's business." A wife is sometimes debarred by a covetous domestic tyrant from giving the ready aid her sympathy and charity would afford.

Marriage should signify a union of hearts. Furthermore, the time cometh of which Jesus spake, when he declared that in the resurrection there should be no more marrying nor giving in marriage, but man would be as the angels. Then shall Soul rejoice in its own, in which passion has no part. Then white-robed purity will unite in one person masculine wisdom and feminine love, spiritual understanding and perpetual peace.

Until it is learned that God is the Father of all, marriage will continue. Let not mortals permit a disregard of law which might lead to a worse state of society than now exists. Honesty and virtue ensure the stability of the marriage covenant. Spirit will ultimately claim its own,—all that really is,—and the voices of physical sense will be forever hushed.

Experience should be the school of virtue, and human happiness should proceed from man's highest nature. May Christ, Truth, be present at every bridal altar to turn the water into wine and to give to human life an inspiration by which man's spiritual and eternal existence may be discerned.

If the foundations of human affection are consistent with progress, they will be strong and enduring. Divorces should warn the age of some fundamental error in the marriage state. The union of the sexes suffers fearful discord. To gain Christian Science and its harmony, life should be more metaphysically regarded.

The broadcast powers of evil so conspicuous to-day show themselves in the materialism and sensualism of the age, struggling against the advancing spiritual era. Beholding the world's lack of Christianity and the powerlessness of vows to make home happy, the human mind will at length demand a higher affection.

There will ensue a fermentation over this as over many other reforms, until we get at last the clear straining of truth, and impurity and error are left among the lees. The fermentation even of fluids is not pleasant. An unsettled, transitional stage is never desirable on its own account. Matrimony, which was once a fixed fact among us, must lose its present slippery footing, and man must find permanence and peace in a more spiritual adherence.

The mental chemicalization, which has brought conjugal infidelity to the surface, will assuredly throw off this evil, and marriage will become purer when the scum is gone.

Thou art right, immortal Shakespeare, great poet of humanity: "Sweet are the uses of adversity; Which, like the toad, ugly and venomous, Wears yet a precious jewel in his head."

Trials teach mortals not to lean on a material staff,—a broken reed, which pierces the heart. We do not half remember this in the sunshine of joy and prosperity. Sorrow is salutary. Through great tribulation we enter the kingdom. Trials are proofs of God's care. Spiritual development germinates not from seed sown in the soil of material hopes, but when these decay, Love propagates anew the higher joys of Spirit, which have no taint of earth. Each successive stage of experience unfolds new views of divine goodness and love.

Amidst gratitude for conjugal felicity, it is well to remember how fleeting are human joys. Amidst conjugal infelicity, it is well to hope, pray, and wait patiently on divine wisdom to point out the path.

Husbands and wives should never separate if there is no Christian demand for it. It is better to await the logic of events than for a wife precipitately to leave her husband or for a husband to leave his wife. If one is better than the other, as must always be the case, the other preeminently needs good company. Socrates considered patience salutary under such circumstances, making his Xantippe a discipline for his philosophy.

Sorrow has its reward. It never leaves us where it found us. The furnace separates the gold from the dross that the precious metal may be graven with the image of God. The cup our Father hath given, shall we not drink it and learn the lessons He teaches?

When the ocean is stirred by a storm, then the clouds lower, the wind shrieks through the tightened shrouds, and the waves lift themselves into mountains. We ask the helmsman: "Do you know your course? Can you steer safely amid the storm?" He answers bravely, but even the dauntless seaman is not sure of his safety; nautical science is not equal to the Science of Mind. Yet, acting up to his highest understanding, firm at the post of duty, the mariner works on and awaits the issue. Thus should we deport ourselves on the seething ocean of sorrow. Hoping and working, one should stick to the wreck, until an irresistible propulsion precipitates his doom or sunshine gladdens the troubled sea.

The notion that animal natures can possibly give force to character is too absurd for consideration, when we remember that through spiritual ascendency our Lord and Master healed the sick, raised the dead, and commanded even the winds and waves to obey him. Grace and Truth are potent beyond all other means and methods.

The lack of spiritual power in the limited demonstration of popular Christianity does not put to silence the labor of centuries. Spiritual, not corporeal, consciousness is needed. Man delivered from sin, disease, and death presents the true likeness or spiritual ideal.

Systems of religion and medicine treat of physical pains and pleasures, but Jesus rebuked the suffering from any such cause or effect. The epoch approaches when the understanding of the truth of being will be the basis of true religion. At present mortals progress slowly for fear of being thought ridiculous. They are slaves to fashion, pride, and sense. Sometime we shall learn how Spirit, the great architect, has created men and women in Science. We ought to weary of the fleeting and false and to cherish nothing which hinders our highest selfhood.

Jealousy is the grave of affection. The presence of mistrust, where confidence is due, withers the flowers of Eden and scatters love's petals to decay. Be not in haste to take the vow "until death do us part." Consider its obligations, its responsibilities, its relations to your growth and to your influence on other lives.

I never knew more than one individual who believed in agamogenesis; she was unmarried, a lovely character, was suffering from incipient insanity, and a Christian Scientist cured her. I have named her case to individuals, when casting my bread upon the waters, and it may have caused the good to ponder and the evil to hatch their silly innuendoes and lies, since salutary causes sometimes incur these effects. The perpetuation of the floral species by bud or cell-division is evident, but I discredit the belief that agamogenesis applies to the human species.

Christian Science presents unfoldment, not accretion; it manifests no material growth from molecule to mind, but an impartation of the divine Mind to man and the universe. Proportionately as human generation ceases, the unbroken links of eternal, harmonious being will be spiritually discerned; and man, not of the earth earthly but coexistent with God, will appear. The scientific fact that man and the universe are evolved from Spirit, and so are spiritual, is as fixed in divine Science as is the proof that mortals gain the sense of health only as they lose the sense of sin and disease. Mortals can never understand God's creation while believing that man is a creator. God's children already created will be cognized only as man finds the truth of being. Thus it is that the real, ideal man appears in proportion as the false and material disappears. No longer to marry or to be "given in marriage" neither closes man's continuity nor his sense of increasing number in God's infinite plan. Spiritually to understand that there is but one creator, God, unfolds all creation, confirms the Scriptures, brings the sweet assurance of no parting, no pain, and of man deathless and perfect and eternal.

If Christian Scientists educate their own offspring spiritually, they can educate others spiritually and not conflict with the scientific sense of God's creation. Some day the child will ask his parent: "Do you keep the First Commandment? Do you have one God and creator, or is man a creator?" If the father replies, "God creates man through man," the child may ask, "Do you teach that Spirit creates materially, or do you declare that Spirit is infinite, therefore matter is out of the question?" Jesus said, "The children of this world marry, and are given in marriage: But they which shall be accounted worthy to obtain that world, and the resurrection from the dead, neither marry, nor are given in marriage."

Parallel Chapter from Eddy's version of *Science and Health*

Chapter IX—Creation

Thy throne is established of old
Thou art from everlasting.—PSALMS.

For we know that the whole creation groaneth and travaileth in pain together until now. And not only they, but ourselves also, which have the firstfruits of the Spirit, even we ourselves groan within ourselves, waiting for the adoption, to wit, the redemption of our body.—PAUL.

Eternal Truth is changing the universe. As mortals drop off their mental swaddling-clothes, thought expands into expression. "Let there be light," is the perpetual demand of Truth and Love, changing chaos into order and discord into the music of the spheres. The mythical human theories of creation, anciently classified as the higher criticism, sprang from cultured scholars in Rome and in Greece, but they afforded no foundation for accurate views of creation by the divine Mind.

Mortal man has made a covenant with his eyes to belittle Deity with human conceptions. In league with material sense, mortals take limited views of all things. That God is corporeal or material, no man should affirm.

The human form, or physical finiteness, cannot be made the basis of any true idea of the infinite Godhead. Eye hath not seen Spirit, nor hath ear heard His voice.

Progress takes off human shackles. The finite must yield to the infinite. Advancing to a higher plane of action, thought rises from the material sense to the spiritual, from the scholastic to the inspirational, and from the mortal to the immortal. All things are created spiritually. Mind, not matter, is the creator. Love, the divine Principle, is the Father and Mother of the universe, including man.

The theory of three persons in one God (that is, a personal Trinity or Tri-unity) suggests polytheism, rather than the one ever-present I AM. "Hear, O Israel: the Lord our God is one Lord."

The everlasting I AM is not bounded nor compressed within the narrow limits of physical humanity, nor can He be understood aright through mortal concepts. The precise form of God must be of small importance in comparison with the sublime question, What is infinite Mind or divine Love?

Who is it that demands our obedience? He who, in the language of Scripture, "doeth according to His will in the army of heaven, and among the inhabitants of the earth; and none can stay His hand, or say unto Him, What doest Thou?"

No form nor physical combination is adequate to represent infinite Love. A finite and material sense of God leads to formalism and narrowness; it chills the spirit of Christianity.

A limitless Mind cannot proceed from physical limitations. Finiteness cannot present the idea or the vastness of infinity. A mind originating from a finite or material source must be limited and finite. Infinite Mind is the creator, and creation is the infinite image or idea emanating from this Mind. If Mind is within and without all things, then all is Mind; and this definition is scientific.

If matter, so-called, is substance, then Spirit, matter's unlikeness, must be shadow; and shadow cannot produce substance. The theory that Spirit is not the only substance and creator is pantheistic heterodoxy, which ultimates in sickness, sin, and death; it is the belief in a bodily soul and a material mind, a soul governed by the body and a mind in matter. This belief is shallow pantheism.

Mind creates His own likeness in ideas, and the substance of an idea is very far from being the supposed substance of non-intelligent matter. Hence the Father Mind is not the father of matter. The material senses and human conceptions would translate spiritual ideas into material beliefs, and would say that an anthropomorphic God, instead of infinite Principle,—in other words, divine Love,—is the father of the rain, "who hath begotten the drops of dew," who bringeth "forth Mazzaroth in his season," and guideth "Arcturus with his sons."

Finite mind manifests all sorts of errors, and thus proves the material theory of mind in matter to be the antipode of Mind. Who hath found finite life or love sufficient to meet the demands of human want and woe,—to still the desires, to satisfy the aspirations? Infinite Mind cannot be limited to a finite form, or Mind would lose its infinite character as inexhaustible Love, eternal Life, omnipotent Truth.

It would require an infinite form to contain infinite Mind. Indeed, the phrase *infinite form* involves a contradiction of terms. Finite man cannot be the image and likeness of the infinite God. A mortal, corporeal, or finite conception of God cannot embrace the glories of limitless, incorporeal Life and Love. Hence the unsatisfied human craving for something better, higher, holier, than is afforded by a material belief in a physical God and man. The insufficiency of this belief to supply the true idea proves the falsity of material belief.

Man is more than a material form with a mind inside, which must escape from its environments in order to be immortal. Man reflects infinity, and this reflection is the true idea of God.

God expresses in man the infinite idea forever developing itself, broadening and rising higher and higher from a boundless basis. Mind manifests all that exists in the infinitude of Truth. We know no more of man as the true divine image and likeness, than we know of God.

The infinite Principle is reflected by the infinite idea and spiritual individuality, but the material so-called senses have no cognizance of either Principle or its idea. The human capacities are enlarged and perfected in proportion as humanity gains the true conception of man and God.

Mortals have a very imperfect sense of the spiritual man and of the infinite range of his thought. To him belongs eternal Life. Never born and never dying, it were impossible for man, under the government of God in eternal Science, to fall from his high estate.

Through spiritual sense you can discern the heart of divinity, and thus begin to comprehend in Science the generic term *man*. Man is not absorbed in Deity, and man cannot lose his individuality, for he reflects eternal Life; nor is he an isolated, solitary idea, for he represents infinite Mind, the sum of all substance.

In divine Science, man is the true image of God. The divine nature was best expressed in Christ Jesus, who threw upon mortals the truer reflection of God and lifted their lives higher than their poor thought-models would allow,—thoughts which presented man as fallen, sick, sinning, and dying. The Christlike understanding of scientific being and divine healing includes a perfect Principle and idea,—perfect God and perfect man,—as the basis of thought and demonstration.

If man was once perfect but has now lost his perfection, then mortals have never beheld in man the reflex image of God. The *lost* image is no image. The true likeness cannot be lost in divine reflection. Understanding this, Jesus said: "Be ye therefore perfect, even as your Father which is in heaven is perfect."

Mortal thought transmits its own images, and forms its offspring after human illusions. God, Spirit, works spiritually, not materially. Brain or matter never formed a human concept. Vibration is not intelligence; hence it is not a creator. Immortal ideas, pure, perfect, and enduring, are transmitted by the divine Mind through divine Science, which corrects error with truth and demands spiritual thoughts, divine concepts, to the end that they may produce harmonious results.

Deducing one's conclusions as to man from imperfection instead of perfection, one can no more arrive at the true conception or understanding of man, and make himself like it, than the sculptor can perfect his outlines from an imperfect model, or the painter can depict the form and face of Jesus, while holding in thought the character of Judas.

The conceptions of mortal, erring thought must give way to the ideal of all that is perfect and eternal. Through many generations human beliefs will be attaining diviner conceptions, and the immortal and perfect model of God's creation will finally be seen as the only true conception of being.

Science reveals the possibility of achieving all good, and sets mortals at work to discover what God has already done; but distrust of one's ability to gain the goodness desired and to bring out better and higher results, often hampers the trial of one's wings and ensures failure at the outset.

Mortals must change their ideals in order to improve their models. A sick body is evolved from sick thoughts. Sickness, disease, and death proceed from fear. Sensualism evolves bad physical and moral conditions.

Selfishness and sensualism are educated in mortal mind by the thoughts ever recurring to one's self, by conversation about the body, and by the expectation of perpetual pleasure or pain from it; and this education is at the expense of spiritual growth. If we array thought in mortal vestures, it must lose its immortal nature.

If we look to the body for pleasure, we find pain; for Life, we find death; for Truth, we find error; for Spirit, we find its opposite, matter. Now reverse this action. Look away from the body into Truth and Love, the Principle of all happiness, harmony, and immortality. Hold thought steadfastly to the enduring, the good, and the true, and you will bring these into your experience proportionably to their occupancy of your thoughts.

The effect of mortal mind on health and happiness is seen in this: If one turns away from the body with such absorbed interest as to forget it, the body experiences no pain. Under the strong impulse of a desire to perform his part, a noted actor was accustomed night after night to go upon the stage and sustain his appointed task, walking about as actively as the youngest member of the company. This old man was so lame that he hobbled every day to the theatre, and sat aching in his chair till his cue was spoken,—a signal which made him as oblivious of physical infirmity as if he had inhaled chloroform, though he was in the full possession of his so-called senses.

Detach sense from the body, or matter, which is only a form of human belief, and you may learn the meaning of God, or good, and the nature of the immutable and immortal. Breaking away from the mutations of time and sense, you will neither lose the solid objects and ends of life nor your own identity. Fixing your gaze on the realities supernal, you will rise to the spiritual consciousness of being, even as the bird which has burst from the egg and preens its wings for a skyward flight.

We should forget our bodies in remembering good and the human race. Good demands of man every hour, in which to work out the problem of being. Consecration to good does not lessen man's dependence on God, but heightens it. Neither does consecration diminish man's obligations to God, but shows the paramount necessity of meeting them. Christian Science takes naught from the perfection of God, but it ascribes to Him the entire glory. By putting "off the old man with his deeds," mortals "put on immortality."

We cannot fathom the nature and quality of God's creation by diving into the shallows of mortal belief. We must reverse our feeble flutterings—our efforts to find life and truth in matter—and rise above the testimony of the material senses, above the mortal to the immortal idea of God. These clearer, higher views inspire the God-like man to reach the absolute centre and circumference of his being.

Job said: "I have heard of Thee by the hearing of the ear: but now mine eye seeth Thee." Mortals will echo Job's thought, when the supposed pain and pleasure of matter cease to predominate. They will then drop the false estimate of life and happiness, of joy and sorrow, and attain the bliss of loving unselfishly, working patiently, and conquering all that is unlike God. Starting from a higher standpoint, one rises spontaneously, even as light emits light without effort; for "where your treasure is, there will your heart be also."

The foundation of mortal discord is a false sense of man's origin. To begin rightly is to end rightly. Every concept which seems to begin with the brain begins falsely. Divine Mind is the only cause or Principle of existence. Cause does not exist in matter, in mortal mind, or in physical forms.

Mortals are egotists. They believe themselves to be independent workers, personal authors, and even privileged originators of something which Deity would not or could not create. The creations of mortal mind are material. Immortal spiritual man alone represents the truth of creation.

When mortal man blends his thoughts of existence with the spiritual and works only as God works, he will no longer grope in the dark and cling to earth because he has not tasted heaven. Carnal beliefs defraud us. They make man an involuntary hypocrite,—producing evil when he would create good, forming deformity when he would outline grace and beauty, injuring those whom he would bless. He becomes a general mis-creator, who believes he is a semi-god. His "touch turns hope to dust, the dust we all have trod." He might say in Bible language: "The good that I would, I do not: but the evil which I would not, *that I do.*"

There can be but one creator, who has created all. Whatever seems to be a new creation, is but the discovery of some distant idea of Truth; else it is a new multiplication or self-division of mortal thought, as when some finite sense peers from its cloister with amazement and attempts to pattern the infinite.

The multiplication of a human and mortal sense of persons and things is not creation. A sensual thought, like an atom of dust thrown into the face of spiritual immensity, is dense blindness instead of a scientific eternal consciousness of creation.

The fading forms of matter, the mortal body and material earth, are the fleeting concepts of the human mind. They have their day before the permanent facts and their perfection in Spirit appear. The crude creations of mortal thought must finally give place to the glorious forms which we sometimes behold in the camera of divine Mind, when the mental picture is spiritual and eternal. Mortals must look beyond fading, finite forms, if they would gain the true sense of things. Where shall the gaze rest but in the unsearchable realm of Mind? We must look where we would walk, and we must act as possessing all power from Him in whom we have our being.

As mortals gain more correct views of God and man, multitudinous objects of creation, which before were invisible, will become visible. When we realize that Life is Spirit, never in nor of matter, this understanding will expand into self-completeness, finding all in God, good, and needing no other consciousness.

Spirit and its formations are the only realities of being. Matter disappears under the microscope of Spirit. Sin is unsustained by Truth, and sickness and death were overcome by Jesus, who proved them to be forms of error. Spiritual living and blessedness are the only evidences, by which we can recognize true existence and feel the unspeakable peace which comes from an all-absorbing spiritual love.

When we learn the way in Christian Science and recognize man's spiritual being, we shall behold and understand God's creation,—all the glories of earth and heaven and man.

The universe of Spirit is peopled with spiritual beings, and its government is divine Science. Man is the offspring, not of the lowest, but of the highest qualities of Mind. Man understands spiritual existence in proportion as his treasures of Truth and Love are enlarged. Mortals must gravitate Godward, their affections and aims grow spiritual,—they must near the broader interpretations of being, and gain some proper sense of the infinite,—in order that sin and mortality may be put off.

This scientific sense of being, forsaking matter for Spirit, by no means suggests man's absorption into Deity and the loss of his identity, but confers upon man enlarged individuality, a wider sphere of thought and action, a more expansive love, a higher and more permanent peace.

The senses represent birth as untimely and death as irresistible, as if man were a weed growing apace or a flower withered by the sun and nipped by untimely frosts; but this is true only of a mortal, not of a man in God's image and likeness. The truth of being is perennial, and the error is unreal and obsolete.

Who that has felt the loss of human peace has not gained stronger desires for spiritual joy? The aspiration after heavenly good comes even before we discover what belongs to wisdom and Love. The loss of earthly hopes and pleasures brightens the ascending path of many a heart. The pains of sense quickly inform us that the pleasures of sense are mortal and that joy is spiritual.

The pains of sense are salutary, if they wrench away false pleasurable beliefs and transplant the affections from sense to Soul, where the creations of God are good, "rejoicing the heart." Such is the sword of Science, with which Truth decapitates error, materiality giving place to man's higher individuality and destiny.

Would existence without personal friends be to you a blank? Then the time will come when you will be solitary, left without sympathy; but this seeming vacuum is already filled with divine Love. When this hour of development comes, even if you cling to a sense of personal joys, spiritual Love will force you to accept what best promotes your growth. Friends will betray and enemies will slander, until the lesson is sufficient to exalt you; for "man's extremity is God's opportunity." The author has experienced the foregoing prophecy and its blessings. Thus He teaches mortals to lay down their fleshliness and gain spirituality. This is done through self-abnegation. Universal Love is the divine way in Christian Science.

The sinner makes his own hell by doing evil, and the saint his own heaven by doing right. The opposite persecutions of material sense, aiding evil with evil, would deceive the very elect.

Mortals must follow Jesus' sayings and his demonstrations, which dominate the flesh. Perfect and infinite Mind enthroned is heaven. The evil beliefs which originate in mortals are hell. Man is the idea of Spirit;

he reflects the beatific presence, illuming the universe with light. Man is deathless, spiritual. He is above sin or frailty. He does not cross the barriers of time into the vast forever of Life, but he coexists with God and the universe.

Every object in material thought will be destroyed, but the spiritual idea, whose substance is in Mind, is eternal. The offspring of God start not from matter or ephemeral dust. They are in and of Spirit, divine Mind, and so forever continue. God is one. The allness of Deity is His oneness. Generically man is one, and specifically man means all men.

It is generally conceded that God is Father, eternal, self-created, infinite. If this is so, the forever Father must have had children prior to Adam. The great I AM made all "that was made." Hence man and the spiritual universe coexist with God.

Christian Scientists understand that, in a religious sense, they have the same authority for the appellative mother, as for that of brother and sister. Jesus said: "For whosoever shall do the will of my Father which is in heaven, the same is my brother, and sister, and mother."

When examined in the light of divine Science, mortals present more than is detected upon the surface, since inverted thoughts and erroneous beliefs must be counterfeits of Truth. Thoughts borrowed from a higher source than matter, and by reversal, errors serve as waymarks to the one Mind, in which all error disappears in celestial Truth. The robes of Spirit are "white and glistering," like the raiment of Christ. Even in this world, therefore, "let thy garments be always white." "Blessed is the man that endureth [overcometh] temptation: for when he is tried, [proved faithful], he shall receive the crown of life, which the Lord hath promised to them that love him." (James i. 12.)